Steven J. Taylor

Studies in Inclusive Education

Series Editor

Roger Slee (*University of South Australia, Australia*)

Editorial Board

Mel Ainscow (*University of Manchester, UK*)
Felicity Armstrong (*Institute of Education, University of London, UK*)
Len Barton (*Institute of Education, University of London, UK*)
Suzanne Carrington (*Queensland University of Technology, Australia*)
Joanne Deppeler (*Monash University, Australia*)
Linda Graham (*Queensland University of Technology, Australia*)
Levan Lim (*National Institute of Education, Singapore*)
Missy Morton (*University of Auckland, New Zealand*)

VOLUME 50

Critical Leaders and the Foundation of Disability Studies in Education

Series Editor

Linda Ware (*Independent Scholar*)

VOLUME 3

The titles published in this series are listed at *brill.com/clfd*

Steven J. Taylor

Blue Man Living in a Red World

Edited by

Linda Ware and Janet Story Sauer

BRILL

LEIDEN | BOSTON

All chapters in this book have undergone peer review.

The Library of Congress Cataloging-in-Publication Data is available online at http://catalog.loc.gov

Typeface for the Latin, Greek, and Cyrillic scripts: "Brill". See and download: brill.com/brill-typeface.

ISSN 2666-1772
ISBN 978-90-04-47183-2 (paperback)
ISBN 978-90-04-47184-9 (hardback)
ISBN 978-90-04-47185-6 (e-book)

Copyright 2021 by Koninklijke Brill NV, Leiden, The Netherlands, except where stated otherwise.
Koninklijke Brill NV incorporates the imprints Brill, Brill Nijhoff, Brill Hotei, Brill Schöningh, Brill Fink, Brill mentis, Vandenhoeck & Ruprecht, Böhlau Verlag and V&R Unipress.
All rights reserved. No part of this publication may be reproduced, translated, stored in a retrieval system, or transmitted in any form or by any means, electronic, mechanical, photocopying, recording or otherwise, without prior written permission from the publisher. Requests for re-use and/or translations must be addressed to Koninklijke Brill NV via brill.com or copyright.com.

This book is printed on acid-free paper and produced in a sustainable manner.

Contents

Series Introduction   VII
    Linda Ware
Notes on Contributors   XI

Introduction: Blue Man Living in Red World: Essays in Honour of Steven J. Taylor   1
    Linda Ware and Janet Story Sauer

1 Disability Studies and Interdisciplinarity: Interregnum or Productive Interruption?   13
    Julie Allan

2 Logics of Civic Possibility: Exploring the Legacy of Steve Taylor   29
    Ashley Taylor

3 Still Caught in the Continuum: A Critical Analysis of LRE and Its Impact on Placement of Students with Intellectual Disability   36
    Janet Story Sauer and Cheryl M. Jorgensen

4 Exploring the Legacy of Steven Taylor: Editor and "Gentle Anarchist"   65
    Geert Van Hove and Elisabeth De Schauwer

5 To Keep, to Thrive, to Build in Community   80
    Nancy Rice

6 A Bridge Too Far? Teachers and Community Practice   91
    Jennifer Randhare Ashton

Index   109

Series Introduction

> Change is often unpredictable and indirect. We don't know the future. We've changed the world many times, and remembering that, *that history*, is really a source of power to continue and it doesn't get talked about nearly enough.
> REBECCA SOLNIT (2017, emphasis added)

∴

Critical Leaders and the Foundation of Disability Studies in Education aims to formalize the significance of early histories of understanding disability drawn from the scholarship of those who turned away from conventional status quo and pathologized constructs commonly accepted worldwide to explain disability in schools and society. The series begins with recognition of North American scholars including: Ellen Brantlinger, Lous Heshusius, Steve Taylor, Doug Biklen, and Thomas M. Skrtic. We will expand the series to include scholars from several international countries who likewise formed analyses that shaped the terrain for the emergence of critical perspectives that have endured and slowly given rise to the interdisciplinary field of Disability Studies in Education.

Critical Leaders and the Foundation of Disability Studies in Education singles out individuals who began their professional careers in the shadow of traditional special education research and practice. However at an important juncture, each forged a critical turn from status quo beliefs and practices about disability in schools and society. They dared to challenge the inherited orthodoxy of special education and through their individual and collective efforts professional criticism of special education grew in increasing larger circles among like minds. Their scholarship represents a persistent commitment to reconstruct the narrative in schools and society that marginalized children and minimized life opportunities for disabled people. Mapping their efforts over time, these individuals were subsequently distinguished as among the earliest voices of critical special education (Gallagher et al., 2004; Ware, 2001, 2004, 2017).

Each book began as an invited symposia presented at the annual meeting of the American Educational Research Association—beginning in 2012 and continuing to the present. The symposia panelists were invited to consider the influence made by each scholar featured in *Critical Leaders and the Foundation of Disability Studies in Education*.

The series unpacks the insights of these individuals—who initially worked in isolation—unaware of their common interests that would ultimately lead to this collective. Their thinking served as the initial grounding for disability studies in education despite the fact that none such community actually existed until late in the 1990s. Steven J. Taylor offered that many in this circle of critical special educators advanced disability studies in education "before it had a name" (Taylor, 2006, *Vital Questions Facing Disability Studies in Education*). He explained:

> [T]he key themes underlying Disability Studies in Education can be traced back many years before it was identified as an area of inquiry or associated with professional groups, conferences, and scholarly publications. Of course, in earlier times, some of these themes were not fully developed, and their implications not completely explored. Yet, an understanding of the intellectual forbearers of Disability Studies in Education can help us understand more clearly the foundational ideas underlying this area of scholarship. (p. XIII)

Critical Leaders and the Foundation of Disability Studies in Education articulates this history through the remembering, as Solnit suggested, of our history and to intentionally proclaim this history as a "source of power [that] doesn't get talked about nearly enough" (2017). The series weaves across decades to plot the arc of scholarly accomplishment, inviting readers to look back, while also looking forward in an attempt to build a more capacious and generative DSE community marked by its clear divergence from special education. The claim that "DSE is not SPED!" is a familiar rallying cry among our contemporaries, however, few are aware that Thomas M. Skrtic, writing in 1988, suggested that the "alternative paradigm" he outlined would give way to a discernable reorientation that would "produce a community of special education professionals who would think and act in ways substantially different from their contemporary counterparts" (p. 444).

Today, through professional affiliations and publications, Disability Studies in Education authorizes Skrtic's imagined future—a space for professionals who think and act in ways that differ substantially from those who align with special education. We articulate our commitment to:

> [U]nderstand disability from a social model perspective drawing on social, cultural, historical, discursive, philosophical, literary, aesthetic, artistic, and other traditions to challenge medical, scientific, and psychological models of disability as they relate to education. (Disability Studies in Education Special Interest Group, American Educational Research Association)

Disability Studies in Education makes specific the authority of an agenda to support the development of research, policy, and activism that:
- Contextualises disability within political and social spheres
- Privileges the interest, agendas, and voices of people labeled with disability/disabled people
- Promotes social justice, equitable and inclusive educational opportunities, and full and meaningful access to all aspects of society for people labeled with disability/disabled people
- Assumes competence and reject deficit models of disability.

Informed in a myriad of ways meticulously braided back to those who early on voiced dissent, discontent, and disavowal, Disability Studies in Education scholars have authored a resounding critique of education that pushes our thinking beyond the binary of the social/medical model debate located within the contexts of schooling—and special education in particular. Over two decades following on the "official" launch of the Disability Studies in Education Special Interest Group (SIG) in affiliation with the American Education Research Association, and the subsequent convening of the annual/bi-annual Disability Studies in Education conference co-hosted in partnership with various universities nationally and internationally, we advance a persistent critique of: classification schemes; categorization rituals; hostile behavior/reductionist practice; isolated/segregated/separate placements, and the unreflective and pervasive stigmatization of disabled children and youth embedded in the special education knowledge base. Each volume in this series reminds readers of the enduring influence and leadership of these critical special education scholars. Disability Studies in Education scholars whose work is cast within the shadows of this scholarly legacy are indebted to the bold and unrestrained thinking that remains provocative to this day.

Finally, the series aims to encourage future generations of scholars and educators to find their way "back" to Disability Studies in Education foundational knowledge sooner, rather than later in their careers. We recognize that the most courageous work remains ahead for budding scholars as they declare an explicit "anti-special education" focus in their research, scholarship and teaching. Understanding that individuals considered in this series made a critical turn away from the ideology that shaped special education orthodoxy (Gallagher et al., 2004), and as a consequence many mid-career and senior disability studies in education scholars forged a professional identity challenging status quo thinking about disability common in higher education and teacher preparation programs. Readers will find, we hope, power in knowing that perhaps we need not rage against the machine, yet, roar we must.

Critical Leaders and the Foundation of Disability Studies in Education provides purposeful connections to the wisdom and enduring ideas of these critical thinkers to reveal the depth of their imprint on current research in the field of disability studies in education. However, we caution that this series is not to be read as a compendium of their contributions. What we hope to encourage is that future generations of scholars will mine the original works of these scholars and excavate primary source materials in an effort to reinforce and renew the foundation of disability studies in education. It is a movement that will prosper when informed of its complex and confounding roots.

Linda Ware
Editor of *Critical Leaders and the Foundation of Disability Studies in Education*

Notes on Contributors

Julie Allan
is Professor of Equity and Inclusion and was formerly the Head of the School of Education and visiting professor at the Universities of Örebro, Sweden and Stavanger, Norway. Her work encompasses inclusive education, disability studies and children's rights and is both empirical and theoretical. She has a particular interest in educational theory and the insights offered through poststructural and social capital analyses. Julie has been advisor to the Scottish Parliament, the Welsh Assembly and the Dutch and Queensland Governments and has worked extensively with the Council of Europe.

Jennifer Randhare Ashton
(PhD) is an Associate Professor in the Department of Education and Human Development at SUNY Brockport. She teaches future inclusive educators at the undergraduate and graduate levels. Her research interests include examining contemporary P-12 special education and higher education practices from a Disability Studies in Education perspective. She has written several scholarly articles that have been published in the *International Journal of Inclusive Education, International Journal of Whole Schooling, Classroom Discourse, Teacher Education Quarterly*, and the *Peace Review Journal*.

Elisabeth De Schauwer
is working as guest professor in the field of disability studies at Ghent University, Belgium. Her research focuses on intra-actions with difference in (pedagogical) relations. She works closely together with children, parents, and schools in the praxis of inclusive education. For her, activism, research, and teaching go hand in hand.

Cheryl M. Jorgensen
(PhD) worked as a faculty-researcher at the University of New Hampshire's Institute on Disability from 1985 until 2011, focusing on inclusive education for students with autism, intellectual, and other developmental disabilities. Cheryl's current consultation work focuses on school-wide systems change, policy advocacy, professional development, and writing.

Nancy Rice
is an associate professor in the Department of Teaching & Learning at the University of Wisconsin-Milwaukee. She conducts research on special education policy and teacher education in special education. Most recently, her work has

focused on why parents elect to use vouchers to send their children to private schools in Wisconsin. She has a memory of being in an advanced research methods course, taught by Stephen Taylor. One class was devoted to reading and analyzing a stack of 200 pages or more of rejection letters from journals for work he had submitted. He enjoyed sharing those letters.

Janet Story Sauer
is Professor at Lesley University, Cambridge, Massachusetts. She uses ethnography in her research and teaching about the lived experiences of immigrant families of children with disabilities.

Ashley Taylor
is Assistant Professor of Educational Studies at Colgate University. Steve Taylor's work and mentoring facilitated Ashley's critical understanding of her background in adult education and caregiving of people labeled with intellectual and developmental disabilities. Her scholarship bridges philosophy of education and disability studies in education/feminist disability studies. Ashley's recent work appears in *Educational Theory* and *Harvard Educational Review*, as well as *Critical Readings in Interdisciplinary Disability Studies*, edited by Linda Ware (Springer, 2020).

Geert Van Hove
is full professor at the Department of Special Needs Education, Ghent University, Belgium. His field of research is 'Disability Studies and Inclusive Education.' His research projects are focused on narratives of disabled persons and their families.

Linda Ware
is an Independent Scholar and survived a lengthy academic career at several universities from New Mexico to New York. Her publications appeared in prestigious national and international academic journals. In addition to this series, *Critical Leaders and the Foundation of Disability Studies in Education*, she edited *(Dis)Assemblages: An International Critical Disability Studies Reader* (Springer) and is a Section Editor for *Beginning with Disability A Primer* (L. J. Davis, Routledge). Ware happily resides near Santa Fe, New Mexico.

INTRODUCTION

Blue Man Living in Red World

Essays in Honour of Steven J. Taylor

Linda Ware and Janet Story Sauer

> An understanding of the intellectual forbearers of Disability Studies in Education can help us understand more clearly the foundational ideas underlying this area of scholarship
>
> TAYLOR (2006, p. XIII)

∴

In this volume of *Critical Leaders and the Foundation of Disability Studies*, our focus turns to Steven J. Taylor, who's lifework bridged scholarship and advocacy across decades and disciplines in search of justice for people with disabilities. Taylor offers disability scholars, their allies, and students of academe from a variety of disciplines involving people with disabilities a breadth of work that combines theory and practice. Readers will consider the ways Taylor deployed a sociological, theoretical framework to interrupt the flawed logic of special education. This would place him in the company of others to be included in this series including Douglas Biklen, Thomas M. Skrtic, Len Barton, and Sally Tomlinson. Taylor boldly challenged remedial and rehabilitative therapeutic practices, to instead demand a humanistic approach where the humanity of the individual is the starting point to inform systemic and institutional change. The demand followed, that institutions recognize the need to challenge the institutional forces that devalued disability life experiences as less than and disabled people as unworthy others. Taylor would ultimately make the claim that disability studies in the field of education existed "before it had a name" (2006). This was to suggest that the slow march to progress within the academy to create disability studies as a field of interdisciplinary study was predated by critical special education scholars who challenged the orthodoxy of the narrow instrumental approach taken by the field of special education. Taylor is recognized here as among the "intellectual forbearers" who paved the way for the foundation of disability studies in education. In this volume our authors describe Taylor across a wide spectrum from "soft anarchist" to "humanitarian, researcher, and intellectual giant" whose "scholarship and advocacy [was] always in the service of social justice."

While some of the authors in this volume knew Steve Taylor personally as a colleague or student, his mentorship extended well beyond those with whom he worked directly. I (Linda) initially met Steve as a colleague when I taught at the University of Rochester (UR) late in 1990s. He and Douglas Biklen were the first contacts I made when I moved to Rochester. Steve was a Full Professor and Director of the Center on Human Policy in the School of Education when he invited me to provide a guest lecture in his doctoral seminar. One of those students, Nancy Rice, is a contributor to this volume. I was ecstatic to discuss my then nascent pursuit to advance the merger of humanities-based disability studies with the preparation of teachers. Although I certainly valued the sociological framework and social constructionist orientation Taylor had long advocated to interrogate disability, I advocated a turn for educators, to literature and the arts as the core of my earliest conceptualization of transforming education and special education in general. Steve was less supportive of a humanities-based approach, but he listened long enough to encourage a handful of graduate students to stay engaged. This support informed several funded projects funded by the National Endowment for the Humanities (NEH), while I was on the faculty at the UR. At that time, I was also in the early planning stages for an international conference, funded by the Spencer Foundation—widely recognized as the impetus for the development of disability studies in education (Connor, 2012, 2014; Ware, 2004, 2018). That conference brought together area educators, graduate students (national and international) and an international panel of distinguished speakers in robust debate that challenged special education as the default paradigm for understanding disability in schools and society. It was noteworthy that several of my UR colleagues from the departments of English, Art, Dance, Sociology, and Medical Humanities attended this week-long conference, but only one colleague in the school of education. Other teacher educators from New York City and Syracuse also attended along with their doctoral students. Shortly thereafter, I won multiple grants from the NEH that served to strengthened campus-wide interest from humanities and medical school faculty. Although this was not the case among SOE faculty, I nonetheless negotiated administrative commitment from the seventh largest school district in New York state to explore the "transformation" of general and special education curriculum (Understanding Disability and Transforming Schools in Greece Central School District, 1997; Ware, 2003).

Educators and administrators from several nearby school districts also participated, and yet, the UR dean was not swayed when she declined to support my promotion and tenure. The institutional change required by DSE was beyond the imagination of the SOE (Ware, 2002). Fortunately, my conversations with Taylor continued, and he was quick to secure an academic appointment for me at SU as a Visiting Professor in the Center on Human Policy. Thinking as the mentor he was, his concern was that my CV not include any gaps between academic appointments. It was a strategic move that he orchestrated at a time when it was difficult for me to recognize the potential fallout from the denial of tenure. To be sure, Taylor's mentorship served me well, but Taylor was known by many for such support. In this volume, our contributors describe Taylor as a "soft anarchist" (Van Hove & De Schauwer), a "humanitarian researcher whose 'scholarship and advocacy (was) in the service of social justice'" (Rice), and unfailing in his willingness to mentor (Allan). This assessment of Steve Taylor was made all too clear when the public gathered to celebrate his life at Hendricks Chapel, Syracuse University in the months following his passing (2014). Amid the many academics who praised Steve for his unrelenting mentorship, many of us will forever recall the final comments of his friend, TJ Jackson who brought to life a harder crowd who knew Steve as a "drinking buddy" (1/16/15). Jackson's anecdotes were heartfelt, raucous, and narrated from a podium in a chapel, beneath a row of stain glass windows, calling forth his memories in a gravelly voice reminiscent of Tom Waits. His words prompted a swell of gasps that eventually gave way to boisterous laughter. That evening ended with TJ Jackson reminding us of Taylor's "playfulness" our contributors, Van Hove and De Schauwer also recognized, one who always strived to "unmask middle-class/bourgeois-type seriousness."

Over many years, Steve and I continued to discuss my desire to bridge curriculum between the humanities and schools of education, however he was less convinced that humanities-based disability studies held useful currency in teacher education programs. His interest was always turned outward, to society, and the bridging necessary to ensure inclusive social worlds beyond that which appeared to concern humanities scholars. In comments on the DS-HUM list-serve with the thread titled, "Cripping the Middle Ages" (June 9, 2003), Taylor did not mince words when he responded to the call for papers at an upcoming conference at the University of Leeds (2004), posted by Michael O'Rourke who sought participants for a roundtable discussion. Taylor asserted:

> I don't agree with your characterization of Disability Studies. You describe one branch of scholarship within Disability Studies, albeit an important one, identified with postmodernism and literary theory (and cultural studies). However, Disability Studies scholarship is much more diverse and rich. The earliest writings associated with Disability Studies in the

United States were grounded in Sociology (especially the work of Irv Zola and other leaders in what was to become SDS) and History and inspired, to a large extent, by social constructionism (e.g., Berger and Luckmann) and dramaturgical analysis (e.g., Goffman)—not postmodernism. Your characterization also doesn't reflect materialist and political economy perspectives as found in the British social model of disability and American writings such as Marta Russell's work. There's been quite a bit of research and scholarship in policy studies and law as well.

From our conversations, I was well aware that Taylor was unsettled by much of the provocative rhetoric emerging from humanities-based disability studies. In the thread, it was the particular usage of the term "crip." Taylor made clear that "Crip Theory" would not "adequately capture the experiences of the range of people who fall under the 'disability umbrella.'" He was always quick to remind that early conversations about disability from a disability studies perspective found little space for those with "intellectual, psychic, and learning disabilities" (DS-HUM thread, 2003). It was under his direction that SU initially offered a 12-hour certificate of advanced study (C.A.S.) in disability studies. Taylor often explained how a C.A.S. sufficed in those years before SU designed their undergraduate minor in disability studies. He was adamant then, that the academy too often generated new degrees in the absence of ensuring an academic home for those who completed such a program of study. In time, it became obvious that SU held the greatest potential for the development of academic programs in disability studies given SU's long history of alternative exploration of disability dating back to the early 1970s. The "SU Tradition" as it is described on the SOE website evolved as faculty and students explored:

> [M]edia portrayals and cultural stereotypes of people with disabilities, institutional abuse, the social construction of mental retardation, the history of mental retardation, public policy and developmental disabilities, school inclusion, and the experiences of people with disabilities and their families in the community. Much of the research at Syracuse has been based on qualitative or ethnographic research methods, and faculty have helped to popularize this research approach in education and human services. (soe.syr.edu/disability-studies)

Years later, when I nominated Taylor for recognition as the DSE Senior Scholar (2008), he was initially reluctant to accept this recognition in person. He was not one who sought the limelight, and yet his fingerprints are deeply impressed in the work we continue to produce, informed by his insights and his tenacity—and we are forever reminded that disability studies in education, did in fact, exist before it had a name.

I (Janet) first learned about Steve Taylor while in a doctoral program at the University of Northern Iowa (UNI), and like many others I found a home in Taylor's writing that I could not find elsewhere. His work is powerful in its theoretical critique of systems and services for those who were (and continue to be) some of the most marginalized in our society, while it is also accessible and personal. When I read Taylor's (2000) detailed description of the Duke family, what UK scholar Julie Allan in her chapter calls "the gold standard of disability studies in his exemplary ethnography of a family's encounters with disability," I felt like I finally understood what was meant by "the social construction of disability." Through his writing I was able to *see* how people constructed understandings that were intact and fully human, a counter narrative to the ways in which I had been 'trained' as a special education teacher to observe and catalogue deviance; this was a narrative that spoke to me as a new mother of a child diagnosed with trisomy twenty-one, what is more commonly known as down syndrome.

This concept of the social construction of disability is on display in our everyday lives. I (Janet) recently sat in the audience at the premiere performance of Bernard Weinraub's play *The Fall* (2018, Huntington Theater, Boston, MA), about playwright Arthur Miller's son, Daniel, who was born in the early 1960s with down syndrome. Miller is well known for his social activism and plays that challenge audiences to a high moral responsibility. Most Americans read his plays such as *Death of a Salesman* (1949) or *The Crucible* (1953) in high school. Some may be familiar with his film *The Misfits* (1961) that starred his then wife, Marilyn Monroe, or that he was subpoenaed before the House Un-American subcommittee in 1956 about his political views. But few, until recently, know about Miller's son, Daniel, or the lasting and expansive impact Miller's response to having a son with a disability would have on him and his family.

The *Fall* (Weinraub, 2018) is based on a *Vanity Fair* article about Miller's only son (Andrews, September 13, 2007) that was published shortly after Miller's death. The play depicts a hypothetical conflict between Miller's third wife, professional photographer Inge Morath, Daniel's mother, and the playwright, who decided to send his son directly to an institution. According to a review in The New York Times (Jesse Green, June 1, 2018), "Miller did not visit him there or at Southbury Training School — the facility, later exposed for its neglect and horrors, where Daniel was moved at the age of 4. For the rest of Miller's life, he never acknowledged his son publicly, not even mentioning him in his 1987 autobiography. The playbill seems to offer an apology to Miller describing "Down syndrome, then and now" in which it explains that in the 1960's new parents of a child with Down syndrome were typically advised by doctors to institutionalize their newborns. I was born in 1963, the same year the US Department of Health published a study of parents' reactions to having a child with down syndrome in which many reported being told by doctors their child was "better off dead." Decades later, I joined others in the audience that evening who may have wondered alongside me, what would *my* family have done with *me* should I have been born with DS? Perhaps there were contemporaries of Miller in the audience who made the same decision. Or audience members who wondered about their own children or extended family members who may have been subjected to a similar fate. Writing in the playbill, Charles Haugland (2018) describes the impact of institutionalization on the life expectancy of its residents: "The perils of institutionalization with poor oversight and overcrowding was shortening the lives of those with Down syndrome, not the syndrome itself" (p. 13). Haugland echoes Disability Studies scholars like Taylor who for decades have pointed out that the disabling conditions of greatest impact are those based on the decisions and reactions of policy makers and practitioners, as well as all of us living in a society that seeks to decide who is 'in' or 'outside' acceptable norms. In other words, it is the social response to the impairment that leads to systemic oppression and disabling conditions. As a parent, I live inside the truth of this Taylorism.

There is a scene in the play *The Fall* (Weinraub, 2018) in which Morath (the mother) reads the newspaper—an accurate depiction—about the deplorable conditions of Southbury Training School. During this scene the audience around me let out an audible collective gasp of surprise. Morath then admonishes herself for having only just realized how awful things must have been for their son, admitting she hadn't questioned why the staff limited her access to all parts of the campus, that some of it was hidden from view. I realized I was no longer one to be startled, but instead I was reminded that until my doctoral coursework I too might have gasped upon learning about this suppressed part of our history. Like many Americans I had been unfamiliar with the experiences of people with disabilities or their families before becoming a teacher and later a mother. The playbill acknowledges "the shameful chapter of inhumanity and discrimination in our country" (Haugland, 2018, p.13) but says nothing about what we can do to challenge it. The Southbury Training School that was opened in 1940 remains open today despite a decade long inquiry into its practices and "life threatening conditions" (Jonathan Rabinovitz, 1995). Josh

Kovner reported in the Hartford Courant (February 23, 2017) that nearly 230 people still live at Southbury, paying "the 615 full- and part-time state workers still employed at the residential facility $12.3 million last fiscal year." Kovner explains that families and advocates have long argued for its closure and a repurposing of the funds, and says they are bewildered about the silence surrounding this issue. Steven Taylor would not be surprised. Unlike many of the activists of his time such as Miller who worked on behalf of other oppressed groups, Taylor recognized the inhumane treatment of our fellow citizens labelled as disabled and dedicated his lifework toward bringing these injustices to the attention of others.

Taylor's work, and that of contemporary Disability Studies scholars provide a persistent force to practitioners, policy-makers and service providers to re-examine ourselves. Taylor's own doctoral research into state institutions in the 1970s described the work of the "attendants" or what he called the "custodians"; what he witnessed seemed to have a lasting impact on him as illustrated in a subsequent piece he wrote a decade later titled "Observing Abuse: Professional ethics and personal morality in field research" (Taylor, 1987), a piece he co-authored with Robert Bogdan "Defending illusions: The institution's struggle for survival" (1980), and more recently his book *Acts of Conscience: World War II, mental institutions and religious conscientious objectors* (Taylor, 2009). All of these works call into question our country's stated values of equity and democratic principles.

In 1988 Taylor published a paper titled "Caught in the continuum …" that addressed a problem many of us who have personal experience with special education recognize. This article analysed the Least Restrictive Environment principle of what is now called the Individuals with Disabilities Education Improvement Act or IDEA, showing how rather than *abolishing* segregation, the LRE is used to sanctify segregated schooling practices. By adopting the continuum, he argued, we justify the maintenance of a system that relies on the assumption that special education and related services are somehow aligned with particular places which often are thought of in terms of specialized classrooms and schools. This idea is that if you build (or maintain) specialized schools that people will fill them rather than provide services within natural inclusive contexts. The Southbury School provides an example of this conundrum of which there are many other examples across the country, some that draw even less attention outside of Disability Studies in Education. I regularly assign my current student teachers to read this article to help foster critical analysis of the integration of policies and practices that impact the daily lives of young people with disabilities in schools. I am forever thankful to my first mentors in the field of Disability Studies in Education at UNI who introduced me to Steve Taylor. In particular, Chris Kliewer who invited me to recognize in Steve Taylor a teacher who has now become my own students' teacher.

To conclude, we recognize that for many disability studies scholars, whether those who are new to the field, or those who have spent the better part of their career declaring DSE as their academic home (if in name only and not necessarily, institutionally sanctioned), it is difficult to take the full measure of the impact of Steve Taylor's contribution to DSE and even to their own careers. This series aims to provide a glimpse into the work of Ellen Brantlinger, Lous Heshusius, Steven J. Taylor, Douglas Biklen, Thomas M. Skrtic and others—not as the definitive study of these scholars—rather, it is to provide a launchpad for continuing to think through their work as it inspired the next generation of scholars who contribute to this series. Our efforts to archive the individual and collective impact of these scholars is intended to be generative, and relevant for generations to come.

1 Chapter Overviews

Chapter 1—Julie Allan invites readers to consider comparisons of the "developments and tensions" that evolved with the onslaught of early disability studies conversations in the United States and the United Kingdom. Citing Taylor's essay, "Before it had a name: Exploring the historical roots of disability studies in education" (2006), Allan presses readers to probe their own reasons for engaging *with* disability studies and *within* disability studies (emphasis added). She considers the persistent discrediting of disability studies within the academy and the potential for ever creating a legitimate space for the "insider's view" within the academy. Hers is a candid call to resolve the problem of the under-representation of disabled scholars in institutions of higher education, seeking a collective voice to demand from senior scholars much more than a lamenting about the problem. Allan insists that much will be required of established academics akin to the very activism and mentorship Taylor provided without hesitation. Allan pushes the conversation on disability studies across several critiques that serve to remind that the field remains one in the making, and one made stronger by the moral compass that guided the life work of Steven J. Taylor.

Chapter 2—Ashley Taylor who is not related to Steve Taylor, but she is one of the former doctoral students who contribute to this volume posits the question, "Why focus on logics of *civic* possibility in particular?" "Why focus on citizenship and democratic inclusion as organizing mechanisms within Taylor's work?" She explains that Taylor's research can be understood as "focused on social and educational belonging, inclusion and exclusion, and the professional and institutional mechanisms that lead to these phenomena" and places an emphasis on *civic* possibilities because "Taylor's work pushed the boundaries not only of who deserves to be socially included, but more radically, who deserves to be counted as a community builder and civic equal." By Ashley Taylor's account this is an underlying principle of Disability Studies in Education, one that must begin with the "problematic of citizenship itself: How might schools advance valued states of belonging, participation, and humanness?"

Chapter 3—Janet Sauer and Cheryl Jorgensen build their chapter on Taylor's often cited essay, "Caught in the continuum: A critical analysis of the principle of the least restrictive environment" (1988). They respectfully remind readers of the importance of Taylor's insights in that work that remain salient today. These co-authors demonstrate that, in spite of nearly three decades of research into the efficacy of inclusive education showing positive outcomes for young people with disabilities, we continue to find increasingly *more restrictive* justifications being employed by our school systems. They explain how some advocates for inclusion have successfully argued for greater inclusion based on the non-discriminatory emphasis of the American with Disabilities Act instead of IDEA because the LRE principle has been misapplied.

Chapter 4—Geert Van Hove & Elisabeth De Schauwer offer deep appreciation for Taylor's impact on the field of disability studies through a wider lens. "Exploring the legacy of Steven Taylor: Editor and 'soft anarchist'" describes how Taylor's editorial stewardship of the well-established academic journal, *Mental Retardation* (MR)—since renamed the *American Journal on Intellectual and Developmental Disabilities*—changed the approach to the clinical and academic field to broaden its readers' understanding in part by adding the "Perspectives" section and making it more of an applied journal. This section created a space for different points of view with controversial interpretations to be acknowledged in a prestigious publication. The co-authors utilize powerful examples of the critical intervention Taylor provided in his role as editor to legitimize qualitative research and to ensure "possibilities" to find allies among those who researched disability with an unconventional and innovative approach. They resurface the work of many who Taylor published in MR when none others would consider their work. Carole Rambo Ronai (1997), a sociologist who garnered considerable controversy with the publication of "On loving and hating my mentally retarded mother" is just one. Rambo expressed her gratitude directly to Taylor as the editor, for providing the "thought provoking and supportive comments that strengthened this piece."

Chapter 5—Nancy Rice revisits the importance of how society might meaningfully create community in the pursuit of lasting social inclusion. Rice, a former doctoral student of Steve Taylor, adds heft to Taylor's contention that DSE existed before it had a name, as she traces some of the theoretical influences on his thinking. Chief among those with whom Taylor drew upon was Burton Blatt—a mentor, and ultimately a colleague at Syracuse University. Taylor's "intellectual geneaology," Rice contends, was the filter through which his sociological perspective informed notions of community as more than a geographic/demographic location. His career propelled incredible transformation of both the definition and the provision of services for disabled people that would ensure their right to thrive in "community." Together with his colleagues and co-authors Burton Blatt, Robert Bogdan and Douglas Biklen, this trio of scholars were among those who initially shaped the landscape that became a powerhouse for the study of disability studies at Syracuse University. In particular, Taylor and Biklen probed many of the same social inclusion pursuits that enabled these scholars to "unravel and better understand the meanings of 'mental retardation,' 'care,' 'institutions,' 'friendships,' and 'community life' from a variety of perspectives."

Chapter 6—The concluding chapter in this volume explores the challenge of applying the ideological stance Steve Taylor embraced relative to community building as a central component in a service-learning experience. Jennifer Ashton, a teacher educator who draws from her years as a K-12 educator establishes her disdain for the "faulty logic" of special education as an institution. Like so many teacher educators, Ashton claims a disability studies identity despite her academic appointment in a typical special education program. Ashton holds that her intellectual home is rooted to a disability studies perspective as she strives to create pedagogy and practice aligned with DSE, community-building and service learning. Rather than mindlessly reify the problematic deficit and medical model of disability sanctioned by special education and typical community service-learning program approaches, she imagines otherwise. Her service-learning project was embedded in an introductory required course, that would enable her to "unpack" and "apply" Taylor's influence on community integration. Ashton comes "clean" as she recognizes the shortcomings in her initial program design and informed by *re-reading* Taylor and her own immersion in his ideology, she pivots her program design to align with his values—to the greatest degree possible. This reflection is an honest, articulation of the difficulty of problem-solving a program that rests within a community where exclusion is the norm and special education ideology is firmly set as the foundation.

Authors' Note

"Blue Man Living in a Red World" is the title of the painting that appears on the cover of this book—a work completed in 2013—by his life partner and wife, Elizabeth Edinger.

References

Andrews, L. (2007, September 13). Arthur Miller's missing act. *Vanity Fair.* https://www.vanityfair.com/culture/2007/09/miller200709

Bogdan, R., & Taylor, S. J. (1980). Defending illusions: The institution's struggle for survival. *Human Organization: Journal for the Society of Applied Anthropology, 39*(3), 209–218. https://doi.org/10.17730/humo.39.3.b28j2m175m22077w

Connor, D. J. (2012). *History of disability studies in education.* http://www.hunter.cuny.edu/conferences/dse-2012/history-of-disability-studies-in-education

Connor, D. J. (2014). The Disability Studies in Education annual conference: Exploration of working within and against special education. *Disability Studies Quarterly.* http://dsq-sds.org/article/view/4257/3597

Haughland, C. (2018). Bernard Weinraub's fall: A new lens on Arthur Miller. *Playbill.* huntingtontheatre.org/articles/fall-articles/Gallery/a-new-lens-on-arthur-miller/

Kovner, J. (2017). At $12.3 million, Southbury Training School OT continues to rile advocates, parents. *The Hartford Courant.* http://www.courant.com/community/southbury/hc-dds-overtime-southbury--20170222-story.html

Miller, A. (1949). *Death of a salesman.* New York City.

Miller, A. (1953). *The crucible.* Directed by J. Harris. Martin Beck Theatre, Seven Arts Production.

Miller, A. (1961). *The misfits.* Methuen Publishing.

Rabinovitz, J. (1995). U.S. assails an institution for the retarded. *New York Times.* https://www.nytimes.com/1995/04/18/nyregion/us-assails-an-institution-for-the-retarded.html

Ronai Rambo, C. (1997). On loving and hating my mentally retarded mother. *Mental Retardation, 35*(6), 417–432.

Taylor, S. J., & Bogdan, R. (1987). Observing abuse: Professional ethics and personal morality in field research. *Qualitative Sociology, 10*(3), 288–302.

Taylor, S. J. (1988). Caught in the continuum: A critical analysis of the principle of the least restrictive environment. *Journal of the Association for the Intellectually Handicapped, 13*(1), 41–53.

Taylor, S. J. (2000). "You're not a retard, you're just wise." Disability, social identity, and family networks. *Journal of Contemporary Ethnography, 29*(1), 58–92.

Taylor, S. J. (2006). Before it had a name: Exploring the historical roots of disability studies in education. In S. Danforth & S. Gabel (Eds.), *Vital questions facing disability studies in education* (pp. xiii–xxiii). Peter Lang.

Taylor, S. J. (2009). *Acts of conscience: World War II, mental institutions and religious objectors*. Syracuse University Press.

Ware, L. (2003). Understanding disability and transforming schools. In T. Booth, K. Nes, & M. Stromstad (Eds.), *Developing inclusive teacher education* (pp. 146–165). Routledge/Falmer.

Ware, L. (2004). *Ideology and the politics of (in)exclusion*. Peter Lang.

Ware, L. (2018). Disability studies in K-12 education. In L. J. Davis (Ed.), *Beginning with disability: A primer* (pp. 259–268). Routledge.

Weinraub, B. (2018). *The fall.* Directed by P. DuBois. Hunting Theatre Company.

CHAPTER 1

Disability Studies and Interdisciplinarity

Interregnum or Productive Interruption?

Julie Allan

This chapter considers the positioning of disability studies, by its own exponents and others, as a discipline in its own right and in relation to other disciplines. It draws on Taylor's (2006) historical analysis of the development of disability studies and disability studies in education, which demonstrates how the early critiques of labelling, stigmatization, and the medicalization of deviance has formed the basis of what we today know as disability studies. Taylor's ethnographic analysis of a family's encounters with disability, an exemplar of disability studies, is also examined.

The chapter offers some comparisons of the developments and tensions within disability studies in the United States and the United Kingdom, some of which have arisen from the diverse perspectives and theoretical orientations that comprise it (Taylor, 2006). It explores questions of voice and power that have arisen through efforts to articulate and position disability studies as a distinctive field and in relation to other disciplines. It also considers the boundary work undertaken on behalf of disability studies and the consequences of some of its more policing-oriented manifestations. The extent to which disability studies has functioned as an inter-regnum, marking a gap between disciplines; a more productive form of interruption, which forces an interrogation of particular disciplines; or merely another kind of disciplining, is examined. The chapter concludes with a discussion of the prospects and possibilities for disability studies to become the "default paradigm" (Ware & Valle, 2009, p. 113) and the implications of this for the scholars who choose to engage with and within it.

1   Not Another Tale of Development: Disability Studies Today

Steve Taylor (2011) points out that it is easier to determine what disability studies is *not;* for example, specifically not special education and not rehabilitation. Linton (1998a) also found the *not* distinction useful, marking a border between the socio-political study of disability and the more traditional interventionist studies and calling the latter "Not disability studies." Nevertheless, Taylor identifies the crucial element distinguishing disability studies from other modes of inquiry, namely the recognition of disability as a social phenomenon, and helpfully shows how we arrived at what we today call disability studies. He offers a sociological lineage of deviance studies from the 1960s (Becker, 1963; Goffman, 1961, 1963; Scheff, 1966; Scott, 1969; Mercer, 1969) that challenged the "nonsense questions" (Mercer, 1969, p. 1) about the incidence and prevalence of disability and asserts that:

> ... mental retardation is a social construction or a concept which exists in the minds of the "judges" rather than in the minds of the "judged" ... A mentally retarded person is one who has been labeled as such according to rather arbitrarily created and applied criteria. (Bogdan & Taylor, 1976, p. 47)

Disability studies was formally given a status through the establishment of the Society for Disability Studies (SDS) in 1982 (Connor et al., 2008). Taylor notes the proliferation of disability studies programmes within the United States and offers a justification for this by pointing out that disability is part of the human condition and will touch almost everyone at some point in their lives. He also argues, however, that disability studies has the capacity to analyse every cultural and social aspect of life, from conceptions of normalcy to stereotyping and exclusion. Disability studies in education came to focus on the school's role in constructing disability, identifying the phenomenon of the "six-hour retarded child," whereby a child was only retarded within the context of school and on the basis of an IQ score (Taylor, 2006), and questioned the legitimacy of segregation. Connor et al. (2008, p. 444) note the significance of the formation, in 2000, of the Disability Studies in Education Special Interest Group (SIG) within the American Educational Research Association for giving a voice to those educational researchers discouraged by the "insularity of special education's traditionalism." Disability studies in education has consistently delivered "fearless critiques of special education" (Connor, 2013, p. 1229) that are defensible on account of their rigour and purposeful with their regard—always—for the disenfranchised and disadvantaged Other. They have succeeded in "rewriting ... discourses of disability" (Ferri, 2008, p. 420) and have managed to "talk back to forces in education that undermine inclusive values" (Connor et al., p. 455). However, these successes have been accompanied by an awareness of the power of the orthodoxy to prevail.

Taylor notes that Dunn's (1968) article, "Special Education for the Mildly Retarded: Is Much of It Justifiable?," marked the start of what was for the special educationists (Kavale & Forness, 2006) a series of attacks on segregation.

The subsequent confrontations between special educationists and so-called inclusionists have involved accusations by each side that the other is being "ideological" (Brantlinger, 1997), with even challenges of "heresy" issued against Danforth and Morris (2006, p. 135). These somewhat unsophisticated attacks in which the opponents merely trade insults and talk past one another (Gallagher, 1998) have led to a continuing enmity between advocates of inclusion and special education that seems incapable of resolution.

While in the United States these ideologically "inspired" confrontations have continued to shape the place and function of disability studies, the field of disability studies in the United Kingdom has been characterised by internal tensions, with some significant confrontations between the key proponents. Connor et al. (2008) mark the emergence of disability studies within the United Kingdom from the publication by the disability activist group, the Union of the Physically Impaired against Segregation, of the *Fundamental Principles of Disability* (UPIAS, 1975). Some of the early disputes within the U.K. disability studies field centred on questions of authority and who had the right to speak about disability; others raised challenges about the place of the body in debates about disability and about the "orthodoxy" of the social model of disability (Shakespeare, 2006). In a head-to-head between Mike Oliver and Tom Shakespeare, the utility of the social model of disability, introduced by Oliver and Finkelstein in the 1990s, was brought into question with Shakespeare (2006, p. 9) arguing that disability studies within in the United Kingdom had reached an "impasse" and that what has caused it to become "stagnated" (p. 1), the social model, should be abandoned:

> Alone amongst radical movements, the UK disability rights tradition has, like a fundamentalist religion, retained its allegiance to a narrow reading of its founding assumptions. (Shakespeare, 2006, p. 34)

Oliver responded by denouncing this view and the book in which it featured as "a mish mash of contradictory perspectives" (Oliver, 2007, p. 230).

Steve Taylor (2000) provides us with the gold standard of disability studies in his exemplary ethnography of a family's encounters with disability. Taylor recounts the family's success in eluding stigmatizing and pathologizing constructions of them, through their own immediate and extended networks and through their avoidance of the more austere institutions and facilities "that engulf people in a separate subculture" (Taylor, 2000, p. 87). Taylor describes how the more he came to know the family, the more he realised that the questions precipitated by the stigma-oriented studies of the 1960s were not meaningful. He understood that their world was not constructed in opposition to, nor reproductive of, prevailing notions of stigma, but was a collaborative world that they both belonged to and constructed.

The family studied by Taylor, the Dukes, was described officially with labels of disability, mental retardation, or mental illness, with the head of the family, Bill, depicted by his state special school as a product of cultural-familial mental retardation (Taylor, 2000, p. 70). Taylor, however, revealed how the master status that operated for the Dukes was familial, daughter, sister, and so on, not that imposed by institutions through labels, and family kinship helped to shape social identities and formed strong social bonds. These strong social identities enabled the family members to engage with the institutional labels used on them without being defined or damaged by them: "… the Duke family experience shows that small worlds can exist that do not simply reproduce the broader social contexts in which they are embedded" (Taylor, 2000, p. 84). Taylor showed the stark contrast between the familial identities and those constructed by the official identities and identified four ways in which the family was able to avoid "the stigma and stained identities" of disability. First, the unit of the family served to interpret and organise everyday meanings, away from institutional constructions; second, the family network was extended and broad, with concomitant resources to draw upon; third, the family was entirely separate from those institutions, agencies, and organisations and from their attendant subculture; and fourth, the family members had acquired extensive competence, not discernible through standardised tests in literacy or numeracy, but nevertheless allowing them to function effectively in the world. This plausible counter-narrative to those that "dehumanize" (Bogdan & Taylor, 1989, p. 146) and lead to an "underdevelopment of … consciousness" (Zola, 2003, p. 243) underlines the potency and potential of disability studies.

At the same time as there has been a growth in disability studies that seek to undermine the pathologizing and segregating of individuals, there has been what Hacking (2010) refers to as a "boom industry" in autism narrative, with autism the "pathology of our decade" (p. 633). He expresses greatest concern about the proliferation of fictional accounts, suggesting that these have contributed to forming a language with which to talk about autism. This "language-creation" (Hacking, 2010, p. 637) plays an important role in helping "neurotypicals" (p. 637), which is how some autism advocacy groups have described ordinary, non-disabled people, understand more about the lives and experiences of autistic people. However, as Hacking points out, it also feeds a fear and a fascination with the odd and leaves a sense of knowing autistic people in some universal way.

The global emergence of a more critical form of disability studies is noted by Dan Goodley (2013), who has of course been part of such a movement. This surfaced in response to a frustration with the materialist conceptions of disability studies, stemming from Marxist sociological interpretations, and their limited analytical capacity. Critical disability studies has also reinscribed the body in analyses of disability and utilised embodiment and the impaired body to force an examination of hetero-normativity. A centering of the disabled person has been effected coincidentally with the construction of the non-disabled person (Linton, 1998b, p. 14), "in order to look at the world from the inside out." Goodley (2013) acknowledges concerns that, in becoming critical, disability studies may have become too much of an academic discipline and lost its political imperatives and its anchoring. He does suggest, however, that the logical next step for disabled people and their allies might be to unpack the complexity of disability.

2 Disciplining Disability Studies

Hacking (2011), who declares himself a "complacent disciplinarian" (p. 1) offers a cautionary note about the engagement with one's discipline, based on his experience of individuals who have been oppressed by disciplines, that is, bullied by superiors into maintaining traditional structures of inquiry. His most direct experience of this comes from his own discipline of analytic philosophy, where junior scholars are afraid and are denied qualifications and jobs if they do not conform to the narrow conception of philosophy held by many of its gatekeepers.

The disciplining of disability studies, in the United States, the United Kingdom, and elsewhere, has come from multiple directions: internally, from within its own field; from within academia; and from other disciplines, through enjoinders to undertake inter-disciplinary work. Whilst seeking to avoid the error of reification, I will consider how each of these disciplining forces works upon disability studies and its offspring, disability studies in education and critical disability studies, and reflect on their effects.

2.1 *External Censure*

Disability studies still struggles for acceptance as a serious discipline inside the academy. This struggle goes beyond any effects of the "dis-ing" of disability studies by the special educationists, but includes their efforts at disavowal. Lenny Davis (2013) recounts, albeit gleefully, the putdowns of his work by the medical establishment that draw attention to his literature, rather than scientific, qualifications. Kaufmann (2015) rails against the celebratory or over-positive language used within disability studies, emphasising that some impairments are undesirable, and suggests that in particular emotional and behavioural difficulties (EBD) is "actually something that is not so good to have" (p. 170). He goes further to suggest that some kinds of culture may be negative and indirectly criticises the disability studies practitioners for apparently regarding "any cultural difference as sacrosanct" (p. 173) and for actively preventing prevention, by only allowing intervention for "advanced cases or disasters" (p. 173). Whilst an attack of this kind may provoke mere irritation at its repetition and lack of foundation, it is nevertheless important to acknowledge the continued need for reproach from the special school yard.

A more significant critique, particularly of critical disability studies, has come from Simo Vehmas and Nick Watson (2014), writers about disability who nevertheless choose to distance themselves at least from the more recent developments within disability studies. They argue that critical disability studies raises ethical issues and insinuates normative judgements without providing supporting ethical arguments and regard this failure to do so as morally irresponsible. They also argue that the concentration on how disabled people are categorised and labelled is inconsequential and demand both a "proper metric of justice" (p. 643) and a recognition of the negative nature of some impairments.

2.2 *Insider Lament*

Disability studies in education, whilst clearly still a discipline in development, has something of an exalted status and is protected vigorously and subject to its own self-discipline. The protectors of disability studies, guardians rather than police, assume an authority on behalf of the discipline and those who have experienced its effects are not exactly "flogged by [its] institutional structures" (Hacking, 2008, p. 1) but may be kept outside and denied membership. Disability studies in education appears to exist and function as a semi-private club, with activities centred mainly around conference events. At these events, the successes of the discipline and its members are celebrated, rather than any achievements in tackling inequalities. As someone who has been inside, and part of, this process, this is not an easy criticism to offer, but it seems nevertheless to be an important one.

Connor, Gabel, Gallagher, and Morton (2008) articulate some of the tensions produced within disability studies in education—by its own members. They describe how in the early days, much time and effort was spent in articulating what it was *not*, outlining its presence in relation to what was perceived as absent. The creation of this negative space was important in protecting the members from what was seen as a major threat—from researchers practising traditional special education but who were looking to rebadge their work under the more apparently respectable title of disability studies in education. There was, therefore, a genuinely good reason for guarding the gates; there was also an urgent need to define the essence and mission of disability studies in education. This created some challenges, but also brought a recognition that plurality was a significant, and possibly necessary, feature of both disability studies and disability studies in education. Steve Taylor (2006, p. xiii) underlines this:

> Neither Disability Studies nor Disability Studies in Education represents a unitary perspective. Scholarship in these areas includes social constructionist or interpretivist, materialist, postmodernist, poststructuralist, legal, and even structural—functionalist perspectives and draws on disciplines as diverse as sociology, literature, critical theory, economics, law, history, art, philosophy, and others.

This plurality does, of course, invite scorn from the special educationists; it also creates an assumption that those carefully guarded gates will be opened, from the inside.

2.3 Inter-Regnum

The final mode of disciplining the discipline of disability studies has been through the insertion of an "inter-regnum" (Hartley, 2009, p. 127) and an expectation that disability studies will work with and between other disciplines. The language of public services is becoming similarly infused with the prefixes "inter," "multi," and "co," and forced upon professionals along with the enjoinder that they should work together. And, of course, increasingly there is an obligation to undertake analyses of oppressions that are intersectional, without any clear indication of how these might be achieved. Hartley (2009) points out that the "inter-regnum" (p. 127) within the public services disturbs accepted understandings about school and expectations of professionals and blurs the distinction between consumer and provider. Inclusion, in this new configuration, is thus a shared responsibility, among professionals and involving parents, and one where the lines of accountability are (even) less clear. Similarly, we might suspect that the inter-regnum in relation to other disciplines or to other arenas of oppression could effect a similar blurring or could merely allow a dominance of the more powerful voices.

Hacking (2008) records his suspicion of the inter-regnum visited upon disciplines and seeks to speak up for collaborating disciplines that do not necessarily need to be interdisciplinary. He suggests that one way to be interdisciplinary is simply to be curious about everything and to be 'disciplined enough to pick up what is going on in other disciplines' (Hacking, 2011, p. 1). He appears to be discouraging any interdisciplinary aspirations, advocating collaboration over interdisciplinary work, and characterising the former by an openness, curiosity, and mutual respect:

> In my opinion what matters is that honest and diligent thinkers and activists respect each other's learned skills and innate talents. Who else to go to but someone who knows more than you do, or can do something better than you can? Not because you are inexpert in your domain, but because you need help from another one. I never seek help from an "interdisciplinary" person, but only from a "disciplined" one. Never? Well, hardly ever. (Hacking, 2008, p. 5)

Hacking strongly recommends a combination of curiosity and discipline, the latter inspired for him by Leibnitz, and avoiding the creation of disciples. In the final section of this chapter, I offer some reflections on the prospects and possibilities for disability studies as an inevitable and obvious form of scholarship.

3 Disability Studies by Default

Linda Ware (2001) issued the challenge, "Dare we do disability studies?" (p. 107), demanding that disability be "thought and thought otherwise" (p. 112) and, in so doing, underlined the requirements for boldness, tenacity, and even humour. Ware and Valle (2009, p. 113) also argued that disability studies should become the "default paradigm," a necessity particularly within teacher education, to "dislodge the silence buried deep within the uninspired curriculum that restricts teacher and student imagination" (Ware, 2001, p. 120). Bogdan and Taylor (1989) see the recognition of the humanness of severely disabled people, achieved through disability studies, as an act of humanity in itself and argue that it is not a matter of individuals' physical or mental condition but a "matter of definition" (p. 146). Goodley (2014, p. xvi) suggests that the crucial function of disability studies is the help it offers to the "normal" to move out of their "normative shadows" and calls for a politics of abnormality to be embedded within disability studies.

In considering how we might go on with disability studies, some attention to the space in which it takes place, the people involved, and the work undertaken seems timely, and these are addressed below.

3.1   *The Space*

The space in which we might do disability studies is necessarily one that needs to be created and made to work for us, rather than involving the capturing of pre-existing and inevitably tainted spaces. Goodley (2013), following Lash (2001, p. 641), suggests that such a space should be "lifted out" and should allow simultaneously for thinking, acting, engaging, and resisting, while Latour (2006, p. 248) characterises it as a space of "mediating, assembling, [and] gathering." The space could also be made for demonstration in a way that takes up the "demos," meaning the people, and materializes them through a process of *demos*-stration, "manifesting the presence of those who do not count" (Critchley, 2007, p. 130). Arendt (1958, p. 198) advocates seeking out spaces for public action, suggesting that these may be anywhere and invoking the *polis* as meaning the "space of appearance" and a space for political action:

> The *polis*, properly speaking, is not the city-state in its physical location; it is the organization of the people as it arises out of acting and speaking together, and its true space lies between people living together for this purpose, no matter where they happen to be.

Arendt extends an invitation to the academic to undertake such political work, but recognizes that academe has never succeeded in achieving Plato's vision of being a "counter-society" (2006, p. 256). Nevertheless, the civic responsibilities of academics for "pricking the consciousness of the public" (Zola, 2003, p. 10) are clear.

3.2   *The People*

In spite of Simi Linton's (1998a, p. 538) enjoinder to non-academics to challenge the "minimal presence of disabled scholars in their institutions," there is still an under-representation of disabled scholars in higher education. Institutions' equality policies encompass disability but privilege the more visible and measurable gender and ethnicity characteristics. Disclosure of disability within the university as a place of work remains a big deal, especially where this might involve mental health issues. There is much to do in order to foreground the expertise of disabled people in research about disability (and everything else) and in academic institutions generally.

Disability studies is an obvious domain for scholars who want to do work that can make a significant difference and the prospect of joining such an accomplished group will appeal to many. But there are potential risks for early-career scholars entering this particularly charged part of the academy.

Many of the dissenters occupy powerful positions within institutions and can exert influence on dissertation committees and appointment and promotions panels. It is vital that established academics use their seniority to advocate for and support more junior staff and to counter negativity from outside the field. Steve Taylor was exemplary in this respect, described as "quiet yet transformative" (Fujiura, 2015, p. 1) by one of the many scholars he mentored, and Syracuse, under the leadership of Doug Biklen, has provided a particularly nurturing environment for disability studies scholars. Len Barton and Peter Clough (1995) urged academics to consider their power and privilege more generally:

> What responsibilities arise from the privileges I have as a result of my social position? How can I use my knowledge and skills to challenge, for example, the forms of oppression disabled people experience? Does my writing and speaking reproduce a system of domination or challenge that system? (p. 144)

Linda Ware has been a consistent voice in calling for new alliances with academics in the humanities (Ware, 2001) and these disciplines remain our best bet for any kind of meaningful engagement within the academy. But Hacking (2008) encourages a further reach into perhaps unexpected disciplines, guided by curiosity rather than propriety. As has been alluded to earlier in this chapter, Hacking considers it potentially too limiting to call such engagement across diverse spheres interdisciplinary work. He prefers to name it as collaboration, involving not breaking down of boundaries but respect. This is a characteristic of the work being advocated and discussed below.

3.3   *The Work*

The work of disability studies undoubtedly involves critique, whether it calls itself critical disability studies, disability studies in education, or something else yet to be thought of. The academic practising disability studies is, therefore, a critic:

> The critic is not the one who debunks, but the one who assembles. The critic is not the one who lifts the rugs from under the feet of the naıve believers, but the one who offers the participants arenas in which to gather. The critic is not the one who alternates haphazardly between antifetishism and positivism like the drunk iconoclast drawn by Goya, but the one for whom, if something is constructed, then it means it is fragile and thus in great need of care and caution. (Latour, 2004, p. 246)

The purpose of critique is to understand the political ends intended by specific practices and to make these explicit, serving, as Said (1995) suggests, "as public memory to recall what is forgotten or ignored" (p. 5). It is not, as Foucault (1988, p. 154) contends, "a matter of saying that things are not right as they are" but rather "of pointing out on what kinds of assumptions, what kinds of familiar, unchallenged, and unconsidered modes of thought the practices that we accept rest" (p. 155). The focus of critique is principally the under-represented, the disenfranchised, and misrecognized other, with the naming and privileging of their voices and identities, making a discourse of that which has formerly been a noise (Rancière, 2008, p. 3) and producing rupture:

> For me a political subject is a subject who employs the competence of the so-called incompetents or the part of those who have no part, and not an additional group to be recognised as part of society. "Visible minorities" means exceeding the system of represented groups, of constituted identities. ... It's a rupture that opens out into the recognition of the competence of anyone, not the addition of a unit.

The critic wades into the "conflict between truth and politics" (Arendt, 2006, p. 227) and attempts to "find out, stand guard over, and interpret factual truth" (Arendt, 2006, pp. 256–257). However, the critical work invoked here amounts to far more than truth-telling, and is positive and constructive, pointing to new ways of conceptualizing and critiquing disability and new forms of political action arising from this critique.

Because critique involves engaging in exercises in political thought, practice and training is required (Arendt, 2006). Critique, thus, is a form of training that does not prescribe what we should think but helps us to learn *how* to think and offers a fighting experience gained from standing one's ground between "the clashing waves of past and future" (Arendt, 2006, p. 13). This is exemplified in Kafka's parable:

> He has two antagonists: the first presses him from behind, from the origin. The second blocks the road ahead. He gives battle to both. To be sure, the first supports him in his fight with the second, for he wants to push him forward, and in the same way the second supports him in his fight with the first, since he drives him back. But it is only theoretically so. For it is not only the two antagonists who are there, but he himself as well, and who really knows his intentions? His dream, though, is that some time in an unguarded moment ... he will jump out of the fighting line and

be promoted, on account of his experience of fighting, to the position of umpire over his antagonists in their fight with each other. (Cited in Arendt, 2006, p. 7)

A methodology for critique, which enables the identification of erasures, closures, and silences, has been developed by Edward Said (1993, 1999) through an elaboration of the concepts of contrapuntality and fugue, taken directly from Western classical music. This methodology allows for the representation of identity and voice and for the "the telling of alternative stories by those that are currently marginalized and exiled" (Chowdry, 2007, p. 103). It seeks to speak of both oppression and resistance to it, achieved by "extending our reading of the texts to include what was once forcibly excluded" (Said, 1993, p. 67), but recovering these voices and dissonances. Contrapuntals allow various themes to play off one another without privilege being accorded to any one. The wholeness of the piece of music comes from that interplay of the themes, which can be as many as 14, as in Bach's *Art of Fugue*, but with each of them distinct. As Symes (2006, p. 324) notes, "History is a giant fugue of interweaving themes and voices, of subject and reply. A contrapuntal reading of culture entails the entire constellation of its *voices*." Chowdry (2007, p. 105) points out that contrapuntal analysis is more a simple appeal for a plurality of voices, but is a call for "*worlding* the texts, institutions, and practices, for historicizing them, for interrogating their sociality and materiality, for paying attention to the hierarchies and the power-knowledge nexus embedded in them." It is also a plea for the recovery of what Said (2000, p. 444) calls "non-coercive and non-dominating knowledge." A contrapuntal analysis, characterized by "counterpoint, intertwining, and integration" (Chowdry, 2007, p. 107), destabilizes conventional readings and "reveals the hidden interests, the embedded power relations, and the political alignments" (Chowdry, 2007, p. 107).

A contrapuntal analysis of disability would involve a reading of disability as culture and of attending to its practices of description, communication, and representation through which certain narratives succeed in blocking others and whereby particular "philological tricks" (Said, cited in Chowdry, 2007, p. 110) allow disability culture to be rendered distinct from the rest of the world and inferior. Crucially, contrapuntal analysis would also seek out those voices of disability culture "which flow across cultures, that defy space and time, that start local, become global" (Symes, 2006, p. 314). Furthermore, contrapuntal analysis has a particularly exciting potential for intersectional analysis and the interrogation of disability in its counterpoint with race, class, gender, and other forms of oppression. It takes us beyond analyses of oppression, however, by taking us away from the positioning of antagonisms, of "absurd opposition" (Said, quoted in Salusinszky, 1987, p. 147), and of disadvantage always being presented as caused by another's advantage. It offers instead a "mollifying (though note not solving)" (Symes, 2006, p. 320) by allowing different elements to sit in relation to one another in a kind of "fugal resolution" (Symes, 2006, p. 321).

4 Disability Studies to Come

Nussbaum (2006) reminds us that we still lack a theory that deals adequately with the needs of citizens with impairments and disabilities, as most of these are based on political principles of mutual advantage. We lack so much more in the field of disability studies but also have so much to gain and to give. On the matter of giving, Steve Taylor again provides a measure or a "moral compass" (Linton, 2009, p. 1), with the mixture of curiosity and outrage, coupled with the most assiduous scholarship, that drove the production of his seminal text, *Acts of Conscience: World War II, Mental Institutions, and Religious Conscientious Objectors*. Taylor's (2009, p. 382) desire to understand "how society can dehumanize, marginalize, and systematically discriminate against people with real or presumed, intellectual, mental, or physical disabilities" is one that ought to compel us all.

Acknowledgment

This chapter originally appeared as: Allen, J. (2020). Disability studies and interdisciplinarity: Interregnum or productive interruption? In L. Ware (Ed.), *Critical readings in interdisciplinary disability studies, (Dis)assemblages* (pp. 5–17). Springer Nature Switzerland AG. Reprinted here with permission.

References

Arendt, H. (1958). *The human condition*. University of Chicago Press.
Arendt, H. (2006). *Between past and future: Eight exercises in political thought*. Penguin Books.
Barton, L., & Clough, P. (1995). Conclusion: Many urgent voices. In P. Clough & L. Barton (Eds.), *Making difficulties: Research and the construction of SEN*. Paul Chapman.
Becker, H. (1963). *Outsiders: Studies in the sociology of deviance*. Free Press.

Bogdan, R., & Taylor, S. J. (1976). The judged, not the judges: An insider's view of mental retardation. *American Psychologist, 31*(1), 47–52.

Bogdan, S., & Taylor, S. J. (1989). Relationships with severely disabled people: The social construction of humanness. *Social Problems, 36*(1), 135–148.

Brantlinger, E. (1997). Using ideology: Cases of nonrecognition of the politics of research and practice in special education. *Review of Educational Research, 67*(4), 425–459.

Connor, D. (2013). Risk-taker, role model, muse, and "charlatan": Stories of Ellen—An atypical giant. *International Journal of Inclusive Education, 17*(12), 1229–1240.

Connor, D. J., Gabel, S., Gallagher, D., & Morton, M. (2008). Disability studies and inclusive education: Implications for theory, research, and practice. *International Journal of Inclusive Education, 12*(5–6), 441–457.

Chowdry, G. (2007). Edward Said and contrapuntal reading: Implications for critical interventions in international relations. *Millennium: Journal of International Studies, 36*(1), 101–116.

Critchley, J. (2007). *Infinitely demanding: Ethics of commitment, politics of resistance.* Verso.

Danforth, S., & Morris, P. (2006). Orthodoxy, heresy, and the inclusion of American students considered to have emotional/behavioural disorders. *International Journal of Inclusive Education, 10*(2–3), 135–148.

Davis, L. (2013). *The end of normal: Identity in a biocultural era.* The University of Michigan Press.

Dunn, L. M. (1968). Special education for the mildly retarded: Is much of it justifiable? *Exceptional Children, 35*(1), 5–22.

Ferri, B. (2008). Doing a (dis)service: Reimagining special education from a disability studies perspective. In W. Ayers, T. Quinn, & D. Stovall (Eds.), *The handbook of social justice in education.* Lawrence Erlbaum.

Foucault, M. (1988). *Politics, philosophy, culture: Interviews and other writings 1972–1977.* Routledge.

Fujiura, G. (2015). Steven J. Taylor: In memoriam. *Intellectual and Development Disabilities, 53*(1), 1.

Gallagher, D. (1998). The scientific knowledge base of special education: Do we know what we think we know? *Exceptional Children, 64*(4), 294–309.

Goffman, E. (1961). *Asylums: Notes on the management of a spoiled identity.* Prentice-Hall.

Goffman, E. (1963). *Stigma: Notes on the management of spoiled identity.* Prentice-Hall, Inc.

Goodley, D. (2013). Dis/entangling critical disability studies. *Disability & Society, 28*(5), 631–644.

Goodley, D. (2014). *Dis/ability studies: Theorizing disablism and ableism.* Routledge.

Hacking, I. (2008). The complacent disciplinarian. *Interdisciplines.* https://apps.lis.illinois.edu/wiki/download/attachments/2656520/Hacking.complacent.pdf

Hacking, I. (2010). Autism fiction: A mirror of an internet decade. *University of Toronto Quarterly, 79*(2), 632–655.

Hacking, I. (2011). *Who are you? The biosocial being.* http://www.yorku.ca/ioantalk/lecture2011.htm

Hartley, D. (2009). Education policy and the "inter"-regnum. In J. Forbes & C. Watson (Eds.), *Service integration in schools.* Sense.

Kauffman, J. M. (2015). The "B" in EBD is not just for bullying. *Journal of Research in Special Education, 15*(3), 157–165.

Kavale, K. A., & Forness, S. R. (2000). History, rhetoric, and reality: Analysis of the inclusion debate. *Remedial and Special Education, 21*(5), 279–296.

Lash, S. (2001). Technological forms of life. *Theory, Culture, and Society, 18*(1), 105–20.

Latour, B. (2004). Why has critique run out of steam? From matters of fact to matters of concern. *Critical Inquiry, 30,* 225–248.

Linton, S. (1998a). Disability studies/not disability studies. *Disability & Society, 13*(4), 525–540.

Linton, S. (1998b). *Claiming disability: Knowledge and identity.* New York University Press.

Linton, S. (2009). *Press release: Acts of conscience: World War II, mental institutions, and religious conscientious objectors.* http://www.syracuseuniversitypress.syr.edu/spring-2009/acts-conscience.html

Mercer, J. R. (1965). Social system perspective and clinical perspective: Frames of reference for understanding career patterns of persons labeled as mentally retarded. *Social Problems, 13*(1), 18–34.

Nussbaum, M. (2006). *Disability, nationality, species membership.* The Tanner Human Values Lectures. The Belknap Press of Harvard University Press.

Oliver, M. (2007). Contribution to review symposium (untitled). *Disability and Society, 22*(2), 230–234.

Rancière, J. (2008). Jacques Rancière and indisciplinarity: An interview. *Art and Research, 2*(1), 1–10.

Said, E. (1993). *Culture and imperialism.* Alfred Knopf.

Said, E. (1995). *On defiance and taking positions.* American Council of Learned Societies. Occasional Paper No. 31. http://archives.acls.org/op/op31said.htm#said

Said, E. (1999). *Out of place: A memoir.* Alfred Knopf.

Said, E. (2000). An interview with Edward Said. In M. Bayami & A. Rubin (Eds.), *The Edward Said reader* (pp. 419–444). Vintage Books.

Salusinszky, I. (1987). *Critiques in society.* Methuen.

Shakespeare, T. (2006). *Disability rights and wrongs.* Routledge.

Scheff, T. J. (1966). *Being mentally ill: A sociological theory.* Aldine Publishing Co.

Scott, R. A. (1969). *The making of blind men: A study of adult socialization.* Russell Sage Foundation.

Symes, C. (2006). The paradox of the canon: Edward W. Said and musical transgression. *Discourse: Studies in the Cultural Politics of Education, 27*(3), 309–324.

Taylor, S. J. (2000). "You're not a retard, you're just wise": Disability, social identity, and family networks. *Journal of Contemporary Ethnography, 29*(1), 58–92.

Taylor, S. J. (2006). Before it had a name: Exploring the historical roots of disability studies in education. In S. Danforth & S. Gabel (Eds.), *Vital questions facing disability studies in education*. Peter Lang.

Taylor, S. J. (2009). *Acts of conscience: World War II, mental institutions and religious conscientious objectors*. Syracuse University Press.

Taylor, S. J. (2011). Disability studies in higher education. *New Directions for Higher Education, 2011*(154), 93–98.

Union of the Physically Impaired Against Segregation. (1975). *Fundamental principles of disability*. Leeds University Disability Studies Archive. http://www.leeds.ac.uk/disabilitystudies/archiveuk/UPIAS/fundamental%20principles.pdf

Vehmas, S., & Watson, N. (2014). Moral wrongs, disadvantages, and disability: A critique of critical disability studies. *Disability & Society, 29*(4), 638–650.

Ware, L. (2001). Writing, identity, and the other: Dare we do disability studies? *Journal of Teacher Education, 52*(2), 107–123.

Ware, L., & Valle, J. (2009). Disability studies as the default paradigm? In S. R. Steinberg (Ed.), *19 urban questions: Teaching in the city* (pp. 113–130). Peter Lang.

Zola, I. K. (2003). *Missing pieces: A chronicle of living with a disability*. Temple University Press.

CHAPTER 2

Logics of Civic Possibility

Exploring the Legacy of Steve Taylor

Ashley Taylor

1   Introduction

In his foreword to *Vital Questions Facing Disability Studies in Education* (2006), Steve Taylor wrote, "an understanding of the intellectual forbears of disability studies in education can help us understand more clearly the foundational ideas underlying this area of scholarship" (p. XIII). Indeed, Taylor was deeply committed to situating contemporary theorizing and social critique within work, however "out of fashion," that came before. This intellectual history not only enables our generative projects, but reminds us to honour our academic predecessors and our activist forbears. How appropriate, then, to honour Taylor's work and intellectual legacy through a volume dedicated to his scholarship. In this chapter, I recall Taylor's work both in its legacy within our scholarly field and as a continuing activist project. In particular, I argue that, among its many contributions, Taylor's work decisively challenges logics of exclusion employed by educational scholars and public service professionals to justify the outsider status of individuals labelled with intellectual disabilities. In doing so, Taylor advances what I want to call "logics of civic possibility" and democratic inclusion.

2   Civic Possibilities

Why focus on logics of *civic* possibility in particular? Why focus on citizenship and democratic inclusion as organizing mechanisms within Taylor's work? Certainly Taylor's research can be understood as focused on social and educational belonging, inclusion and exclusion, and the professional and institutional mechanisms that lead to these phenomena. His work is most centrally about the processes by which stigmatized, devalued, and dehumanized individuals become non-members of social and educational spaces and about the kinds of relationships that disrupt these processes, however small or imperfect. I emphasize *civic* possibilities, then, because Taylor's work pushed the boundaries not only of who deserves to be socially included, but more radically, who deserves to be counted as a community builder and civic equal.

Those who are familiar with *Acts of Conscience* (2009), Taylor's most recent book, will likely recognize the implications for civic possibilities in Taylor's work. The book explores how particular acts are and are not constructed as civic contributions, whether because the bodies or minds that perform those acts are socially devalued (as conscientious objectors to war) and/or because the acts themselves disrupt the hegemonic values of citizenship attached to a particular view of nation-building. In this and other of Taylor's works, we see a systematic deconstruction of the logics of civic exclusion. To do so, Taylor employed particularly powerful methods of dismantling the logics of exclusion behind the concepts of disability and intelligence, both of which play gatekeeping roles in civic and social belonging. Indeed, Taylor's work shows that the conceptual processes that lead to philosophical exclusion from the realm of citizenship are backwards. For Taylor, the definition of the person, or indeed of the citizen, "is to be found in the relationship between the definer and the defined and is not determined by the abstract meanings attached to the group of which the person is part" (2000, p. 84). Rather than exploring qualifying conditions or delineating competencies in advance, Taylor points to the importance of beginning with the problematic of citizenship itself: How might schools advance valued states of belonging, participation, and humanness? What can be learned from the enabling relationships that already exist?

3 The Epistemic Power of Labels

Importantly, for Taylor, the category "intellectually disabled" reaffirms a stigmatizing and invented social position that is a reflection of *changeable* social norms. In *Inside Out* Bogdan and Taylor write "mental retardation exists in the minds of those who use it to describe the cognitive states of other people … Rather than pointing to a clear and discrete phenomenon, the concept creates the illusion that disparate and amorphous conditions and behaviours are similar" (1982, p. 7). This statement is loaded with affective meaning. It is not merely a scholarly statement of a normative claim—namely that what used to be called MR is a mind-dependent interpretation of reality—but also a statement about power—namely that some *over*-occupy a position in which they have the power to solidify a deterministic category out of descriptions of mental states. *Inside Out* was written over thirty years ago, and yet the work of dismantling the myth of intellectual disability remains an active and critical project of Disability Studies and Disability Studies in Education scholars (e.g. Carey, 2009; Carlson, 2009; Kasa-Hendrickson, 2005; Kliewer, Biklen, & Petersen, 2015). Not only does this clarify Taylor's pioneer status in the field, it also reminds of us of the work that continues before us.

For Taylor, dismantling labels, and revealing the mythic nature of intellectual disability, involves a two-pronged attack. First, it requires revealing the dehumanizing consequences of the label and its construction of target individuals as "other." Second, it involves showing the logical contradictions inherent in the label itself and in its application and practice within social institutions. The latter prong is a particularly sharp one in Taylor's work: it takes aim at the *conceptual flaws* in reasoning about the treatment and care of people labelled with intellectual disabilities and challenges the frequent accusations of ideological bias lodged at those who advance inclusion. In other words, in order to divest from the myth of intellectual disability, we also need to divest in the epistemic power that medical, special education, and social services professionals, as well as lay people, have in defining the meaning of lives of cognitive or intellectual difference. We need to resist and decry the temptations of positivism that promise to validate research, even while they invalidate marginalized experience.

In perhaps my favourite of his articles, "You're Not a Retard, You're Just Wise" (2000) Taylor explores the construction of disability among members of the Duke family, a family experiencing a smorgasbord of labels having to do with social and intellectual undesirability. Taylor observes that the family is quite remarkably successful at "insulating themselves from the messages received from programs, agencies, and schools" (2000, p. 69). The quote that forms the article's title is just one example of the ways in which the family normalized words, behaviours, and abilities that were otherwise, and quite consciously, not part of the larger frame of social acceptability. Says Taylor, "The Duke family experience shows that small worlds can exist that do not simply reproduce the broader social contexts in which they are embedded" (2000, p. 84).

4 Small Worlds of Difference

This respect for and elevation of "small worlds" of difference is an important epistemological stance in Taylor's work. It is also a method of dismantling the presumed-as-static nature of disability as a category, namely the view that one's "condition" is unchanging across social situations. As the Duke family's interactions show, a person's perceived competence—and their actual ability to perform tasks, think, feel, communicate, etc.—is highly dependent on the relational context of which they are part. Further, when reading this article, one is struck by Taylor's ability to weave his clear affection and concern for the Dukes, and his role and responsibility as a trusted advisor, not only with but also *into* his work as a researcher. The article is a testament to the divestment in concentrated epistemic power that I discussed earlier.

In Taylor's work it is not only or always labelled individuals who face the threat of social marginality because of a relationship to cognitive difference. In *Acts of Conscience*, Taylor details, beautifully and with great care, the way that institutional caregivers who supported individuals labelled with psychiatric and developmental disabilities are regarded as social deviants by association, and through their actions of inclusion, respect, and, importantly, opting out of the contemporary norm. The following excerpt from the book is revealing. Taylor quotes from one institutional attendee, a Mennonite conscientious objector who worked at Marlboro State Hospital:

> These were people, and they're people even when they're mentally ill. There was a young man who had a good set of firsts on him ... I went in to get his tray, and he threatened to throw it at me. And I said to him, 'Well, this is your room. I'd like the tray to wash it, but I'm not going to come into your room. You have a right to say who can come in or stay out. It's your room, not mine' ... He didn't let me come in but he brought me his tray. It didn't work in every case, but it's amazing how people want to be treated as people. (Taylor, 2009, p. 219)

This excerpt reveals the fundamentally humanizing possibilities of care even in the context of utter dehumanization. While uplifting, it is nevertheless a reminder of the serious lack of respect, privacy, and humanizing care with which so many people labelled with psychiatric and intellectual disabilities experience. Moreover, as allies for and activists on behalf of institutionalized people, these conscientious objector caregivers faced the constant threat of their own social and civic erasure. Small acts of transformative civic possibility are fragile, momentary, and often unrecognized. But they are far from trivial.

5   Caring Scepticism

Taylor's work contributes to the doing of—and perhaps *undoing*—in and of philosophy, a field in which I found a home while Steve's student at Syracuse University. This tension exposed me to Taylor's caring scepticism but cautious belief in academic change. Taylor's work shows that to avoid logics of exclusion, the trajectory of philosophical inquiry must begin not with abstract normative claims about ability and disability, but rather with the situated experiences of individuals whose socially interpreted characteristics place them on the margins of society. Situated epistemologies ground ethical inquiry. The first-person narrative "provides a platform from which different conceptions of the nature of human behaviour can be given force in both the academic and larger community" (Bogdan & Taylor, 1994, p. 20). This procedural point is both methodological *and* political, and is informed by a deep commitment to the belief that research that confirms and indeed creates exclusions *cannot* be ethical in the proper sense. This commitment, which I inherited from Steve, has gotten me into a fair number of battles with ethical theorists.

Expressly situated epistemologies have historically *not* been the purview of philosophers. Indeed, philosophical inquiry has historically ignored the groundedness of social experiences, seeing it as the task of philosophers to engage in the abstract and socially-disinvested, those realms that feminist philosophers have decried as ignoring the reality that minds have bodies attached to them. It is, of course, a well-documented critique by feminists that philosophy has positioned women as non-knowers because of the kinds of thinking processes and habits that men have associated with their positionality, namely emotion and non-rationality, and because women have resisted seeing themselves as disembodied and socially-removed. On its own this type of philosophical inquiry is, to say the least, "troubling," but there is something at stake that goes beyond and complicates the positioning of women as non-knowers through this discourse. The denial of embodiment and the unfettered elevation of reason have also positioned knowing and knowledge as the realms of the intellectually *non*-disabled and non-labelled. In other words, the marginality of women is at the same time the marginality of people labelled with disabilities—and indeed, both depend on one another. This linkage is utterly apparent in the ways that attributes of psychiatric disability and lowered intelligence are used to disqualify women (and people of colour) from positions of credibility, just as these epistemic denials appear always attached to those who occupy precarious cognitive status (A. Taylor, 2015).

Taylor was, quite fairly, concerned about philosophical work on disability. We had many conversations to this effect, including about our shared experiences with philosophers' (and others') critical responses to our work in disability studies. Taylor's concern, and scepticism even, was well founded. There are numerous examples of philosophers deploying disability—intellectual disability in particular—in thought experiments about the nature of human beings, in the obligations "we" have to animals, even the limits of ethical decision-making in medical contexts (see Carlson, 2009). As Licia Carlson (2009), Eva Kittay (2009), and others have pointed out, this kind of "use" of people as examples for moral inquiry is certainly disturbing in its own right, but is also further othering to people with intellectual disabilities.

What could be empowering, then, about a field of inquiry that reproduces the social and epistemological exclusions of people with intellectual disabilities, whether overtly or through its emphasis on rationality, independence, and argumentation? What I so admired about Taylor is that he not only took me on, took me up, and took me *in* as a philosopher-student, but he quite overtly endorsed and pushed my desire to do philosophical work. Implicit in this, I think, is an acknowledgement of the role of incremental and field-internal change. I think this goes back to the enormity of "small worlds:" what kind of small world could be created within a field that has been so destructive to labelled people? How could this small world be transformative of an entire field? Taylor made me think this is possible.

6 The Work before Us, and the Work Ahead

In Taylor's scholarship, grounding inquiry—philosophical or otherwise—in the thinking, feeling, knowing experiences of people labelled with intellectual disabilities not only operates as a corrective to the exclusion of people with disabilities from knowing, but also creates openings and rifts in the fabric of hegemonic claims to the truth. For my own work, this focus on "small worlds" has been so important. How can we observe the small moments that rupture the everyday aggressions against and exclusions of people who exist in precarious civic roles? What are the moments that are full of enormous potential that can be easily ignored by our epistemic practices? In what ways have I been ignorant of or unable to attend to the small acts and gestures that transform relationships across difference, whether in the classroom or otherwise. Why have I not recognized as disruptive the act of refusal to participate by someone whose life is circumscribed by the regimented practices of group-home life? How significant might it be to observe a non-labelled student ask another, whose speech is hard to decipher, "could you please repeat, I didn't understand." The refusal to acquiesce, the refusal to enter another's space, the refusal to ignore misunderstanding—these rather small acts are in fact rather enormous acts of disruption. When people labelled with intellectual disabilities are so frequently dismissed, when they are seen not to be thinking, feeling, communicating beings, the act of asking for repetition can create radical openings for civic inclusion. This is Taylor's intellectual legacy.

Those people who commit acts of conscience need to be remembered and honored (Taylor, 2009, p. 395).

References

Bogdan, R., & Taylor, S. J. (1982). *Inside out: Two first-person accounts of what it means to be labeled 'mentally retarded.'* University of Toronto Press.

Bogdan, R., & Taylor, S. J. (1994). *The social meaning of mental retardation: Two life stories.* Teachers College Press.

Carey, A. C. (2009). *On the margins of citizenship: Intellectual disability and civil rights in twentieth-century America.* Temple University Press.

Carlson, L. (2009). *The faces of intellectual disability: Philosophical reflections.* Indiana University Press.

Kasa-Hendrickson, C. (2005). 'There's no way this kid's retarded': Teachers' optimistic constructions of students' ability. *International Journal of Inclusive Education, 9*(1), 55–69.

Kittay, E. F. (2009). The personal is philosophical is political: A philosopher and mother of a cognitively disabled person sends notes from the battlefield. *Metaphilosophy, 40*(3–4), 606–627.

Kliewer, C., Biklen, D., & Petersen, A. (2015). At the end of intellectual disability. *Harvard Educational Review, 85*(1), 1–28.

Taylor, A. (2015). The discourse of pathology: Reproducing the able mind through bodies of color. *Hypatia, 30*(1), 181–198.

Taylor, S. J. (2000). "You're not a retard, you're just wise": Disability, social identity, and family networks. *Journal of Contemporary Ethnography, 29*(1), 58–92.

Taylor, S. J. (2006). Foreword: Before it had a name. In S. L. Gabel & S. Danforth (Eds.), *Vital questions facing disability studies in education* (Vol. 2). Peter Lang.

Taylor, S. J. (2009). *Acts of conscience: World War II, mental institutions, and religious objectors.* Syracuse University Press.

CHAPTER 3

Still Caught in the Continuum

A Critical Analysis of LRE and Its Impact on Placement of Students with Intellectual Disability

Janet Story Sauer and Cheryl M. Jorgensen

Abstract

The least restrictive environment mandate of the Individuals With Disabilities Education Act has long been questioned as to whether it has fulfilled the original intent of the law (Nisbet, 2004; Taylor, 1988). This advocacy brief provides an updated analysis of the flaws underlying the principle of least restrictive environment (LRE), a mandate that exists at the nexus of cultural beliefs about disability, the influence of the medical model on special education, and the misguided link between intensity of services and more restrictive environments. We review the origins of LRE, summarize research on the positive relationship between placement in general education and student outcomes, describe six flaws of LRE's grounding in the continuum model of educational placement that sanctions segregation, present data that illustrate little progress over time towards general education placement for students with intellectual disability, and outline some key court rulings about what constitutes the least restrictive environment. In summary, we suggest that segregation of students with intellectual disability results as much from the flawed underpinnings of the LRE principle itself as on the attitudes and practices of those who use LRE as a justification for segregation.

Keywords

least restrictive environment – continuum of alternative placements – Individuals With Disabilities Education Act – special education – inclusive education – intellectual disability

1   Introduction

In 1988 Taylor suggested that although the least restrictive environment (LRE) mandate of the Education for All Handicapped Children Act (EHC) was "extremely forward thinking for its time" (p. 227), it led to problematic policies and practices that work against integration for students with disabilities. Taylor (1988) noticed that the continuum of alternate placements, or the operationalized definition of the LRE, was actually being used to justify more restrictive (and least normalized) placements for students with significant disabilities. Nisbet (2004) revisited Taylor's argument more than a decade later, arguing, "The continuum exists but is subtler, in the background, and spoken in terms of access to entitled or necessary services rather than to specific settings" (p. 232). The change in emphasis, however, did little to change practices, in effect ignoring the growing body of research that supported reforms that would otherwise create a more inclusive and equitable system. In this chapter we build on the work of Ryndak, Taub, Jorgensen, Gonsier-Gerdin, Arndt, Sauer, Ruppar, Morningstar, and Allcock (2014) by describing how the LRE mandate of the EHC, reauthorized as the Individuals With Disabilities Education Improvement Act (IDEIA, 2004) is still used to justify the segregation of certain students despite the accumulated research supporting inclusive education, leaving many children in effect "caught" in a restrictive continuum. We suggest that a radical transformation is necessary to move from the dualistic special/general education system that allows for segregation via LRE to a more equitable system driven by inclusive values and practices that benefit all students.

While notable progress toward placement in general education has been made for some students with certain disabilities over the decades since 1975, students with intellectual disability, and in particular students of color, are still denied access to the general education classroom in large numbers. One reason for this inequity is the subjective nature of legal interpretations of the LRE and confusion over the definition of inclusion, thus allowing for the influence of individual preferences based on values, biases, or habits (e.g., "This is the way we do it here"). For the purposes of this chapter we define inclusion as students with disabilities spending at least 80% of their school day in a general education class (i.e., the "most inclusive" of the IDEA placement reporting categories), but this definition oversimplifies the concept.

The word *inclusion* has become ubiquitous, but its meaning is widely debated. Yell (1998) states while "no consensus exists about the definition of inclusion," the "consistent principles" of federal statutes, regulations, and major court cases promote inclusive educational practices (p. 70). Danforth and Naraian (2015) suggest "inclusion is a complex political project in the schools that requires general educators, special educators, school leaders, and other professional personnel to break sharply with prior beliefs and conventions that justify segregation, rejection, and devaluation of students on any basis" (p. 72). This is because "policies do not exist in a vacuum; they reflect underlying ideologies and assumptions in a society, and it is indeed these ideologies that construe the dynamism that underpins inclusive education policymaking" (Liaison, 2008, p. 485). Such social and political values that are enacted each day in Individualized Education Program (IEP) meetings have influence on an international level (Ferguson, 2008). The LRE decision-making process reflects the different local understandings among individual IEP team members as well as state agencies or organizations. Consider, for instance, that in Massachusetts the Department of Education (2014) equates full inclusion with a child spending 80% or more of her time in a general education classroom whereas the Wisconsin Education Association Council (2014) references Phi Delta Kappa's 1993 bulletin stating: "Full inclusion means that all students, regardless of handicapping condition or severity, will be in a regular classroom/program full time. All services must be taken to the child in that setting." These examples of different interpretations of the same words make the practical implementation of IEPs confusing, particularly when families move between states and the local IEP teams must renegotiate the meaning of the LRE. Because we are an increasingly mobile society, such nuances are particularly problematic (Sauer, 2013).

2 A Brief History of the Least Restrictive Environment Mandate

In this section we provide a brief overview of the legal history of the LRE mandate. In the Supreme Court *Brown v. Board of Education of Topeka* (1954) case, the lawyer defending South Carolina's segregated schools linked the end of segregation for African American children with the "frightening" possibility that sometime in the future "a state would have [no] further right to segregate its pupils on…the ground of mental capacity" (Friedman, 1969, as cited in Kliewer, Biklen, & Kasa-Hendrickson, 2006, p. 164). Turnbull (1982) made a similar point regarding the influence of *Brown* on subsequent landmark cases:

> Based on the findings of fact accepted by the courts, special education was viewed as a separate and unequal system of education…. The parallels of the equal protection case for handicapped students and the findings of *Brown* are striking and are immediately apparent by reading the *Brown* case substituting "handicapped" for "Negro" and "nonhandicapped" for "white." (p. 282)

Buoyed by the *Brown* decision and using the equal protection and due process clauses in the 5th and 14th amendments to the U.S. Constitution, two lawsuits were brought in the 1970s, arguing for the right to a free public education for children with disabilities. *Mills v. Board of Education of District of Columbia* (1972) laid the groundwork for the zero-reject mandate in special education law, ordering that all students with disabilities were to be admitted to the District's public schools. In *PARC v. Commonwealth of Pennsylvania* (1972) the decision of the court clearly stated, "...placement in a regular public school class is preferable to placement in a special public school class...[which] is preferable to placement in any other type of program of education and training" (334 F. Supp. at 1260, as cited in Turnbull, 1984, p. 282). The choice of wording here is important: "preferable" is not the same as "required" and the lack of an agreed-upon definition of LRE is one legacy of the *PARC* decision's vagueness.

Favorable decisions in these cases paved the way for passage in 1975 of the Education for All Handicapped Children's Act (EHA), also known as Public Law 94-142. In addition to its other provisions, EHA required that children with disabilities must be educated in the LRE:

> (1) To the maximum extent appropriate, handicapped children, including children in public or private institutions or other care facilities, are educated with children who are not handicapped, and (2) That special classes, separate schooling, or other removal of handicapped children from the regular educational environment occurs only when the nature or severity of the handicap is such that education in regular classes with the use of supplementary aids and services cannot be achieved satisfactorily. (EHA, Federal Register, August 23, 1977, p. 42497)

Although parents and other advocates were optimistic that the new law would result in significant reductions in segregated educational programs for students with disabilities, Sarason and Doris (1979) were less sanguine about the possibility of this outcome. They wrote "... Public Law 94-142 intends a modest quantitative change and in that respect it is miles apart from the 1954 decision which ruled segregation unconstitutional" (p. 369).

Thomas Gilhool, a civil and disability rights lawyer who represented the plaintiffs in *PARC v. Commonwealth of Pennsylvania* (1972), believes that the intent of LRE has been misinterpreted since the enactment of EHA; an intent that corresponds to our understanding of inclusion today. In a 2011 interview he said:

> There's a preference for the placement of the child in regular education over special education and in regular education or even special education over institutional education or what have you. And that gave rise to what

> is miscalled in the popular parlance, unfortunately, the least restrictive alternative requirement of 94-142, the Education for All Handicapped Children Act. In fact, what that provision says in the Act and the language of the orders in the *PARC* case were suggestive of it was that children with disabilities shall be educated to the maximum extent appropriate with children who are not disabled. And if you pause for a minute and try to get the single phrase that would sum that up it would be integration! Not least restrictive environment. (Gilhool, 2011, p. 16)

In fact, although EHA and its subsequent reauthorizations as the Individuals With Disabilities Education Act (IDEA, 1997) and the Individuals With Disabilities Education Improvement Act (IDEIA, 2004) expressed a preference for general education class placement, the LRE mandate still codifies segregated educational placements for some students with disabilities. Far from requiring that students with disabilities be educated in general education classes, LRE leaves the determination about what constitutes least restrictive to each student's Individualized Education Program (IEP) team. This is problematic because placement decisions are particularly vulnerable to team members' experiences and biases, likely accounting in part for the high variability in placement patterns across geographic areas (Brock & Schaefer, 2015) and when comparing white and non-white students (Harry & Klingner, 2006; Hehir, Grindal, & Eidelman, 2012; Kurth & Mastergeorge, 2010).

When reviewing legislation, it is important to consider the tension between federal law and state and local interpretations (Martin, Martin, & Terman, 1996). The courtroom is where legislation is officially interpreted and policies are then established or modified as a result of the court's judgment. Certain cases are referred to as "controlling cases" by circuit courts in which the standard or precedent is set, often providing complicated compliance tests (see, for example, the four-factor test in the Rachel Holland case in the 9th Circuit in 1994). According to special education lawyer Barbara Ransom (personal communication, February 25, 2015), 75% of definitive special education decisions are made in only a few jurisdictions (e.g., California, Maryland, New Jersey, New York, and the District of Columbia). That means local practices are based on decisions that were likely made elsewhere, for what may be perceived as "good" or "bad" reasons depending on one's perspective regarding LRE. It is also noteworthy to take into account the idea Palley (2006) explained, that individual legal claims in cases involving LRE can work counterproductively to systematic change that would otherwise move us as a nation toward greater equity in affording to all students the benefits from being taught in general education.

3 LRE and the Rationale for Inclusive Education

The arguments against segregated placement and for general education placement come from the original intent of the federal education law and from decades of accumulated research. The introductory language of IDEIA (2004) represents Congress' findings that:

> Almost 30 years of research and experience has demonstrated that the education of children with disabilities can be made more effective by having high expectations for such children and ensuring their access to the general education curriculum in the regular classroom, to the maximum extent possible. (p. 3)

While the wording here emphasizes the "in the regular classroom, to the maximum extent possible," in practice placement decisions are usually influenced by the term used later in the law, "to the maximum extent *appropriate*" (IDEA, 2004, emphasis added), further complicating the discussion.

Research on the educational benefits of inclusive education for students with intellectual (and other significant) disability shows:

- Higher expectations for student learning (Jorgensen, McSheehan, & Sonnenmeier, 2007)
- Heightened engagement, affective demeanor, and participation in integrated social activities (Hunt, Farron-Davis, Beckstead, Curtis, & Goetz, 1994)
- Improved communication and social skills (Beukelman & Mirenda, 2005; Fisher & Meyer, 2002; McSheehan, Sonnenmeier, & Jorgensen, 2009; Soto, Muller, Hunt, & Goetz, 2001)
- More satisfying and diverse social relationships (Guralnick, Connor, Hammond, Gottman, & Kinnish, 1996)
- Optimal access to the general education curriculum (Jackson, Ryndak, & Wehmeyer, 2008/2009; Jorgensen, McSheehan, & Sonnenmeier, 2010; Wehmeyer & Agran, 2006)
- Improved academic outcomes (Cosier, Causton-Theoharis, & Theoharis, 2013; Cole, Waldron, & Majd, 2004; Dessemontet, Bless, & Morin, 2012; Ryndak, Alper, Ward, Storch, & Montgomery, 2010; Ryndak, Morrison, & Sommerstein, 1999)
- Significantly higher scores on academic achievement tests for students with autism included in general education when compared to students with autism in self-contained settings (Kurth & Mastergeorge, 2010)
- Improved adult outcomes in the areas of post-secondary education, employment, and independence (Ryndak, Alper, Hughes, & McDonnell,

2012; Taylor, West, & Smith, 2006; Test, Mazzotti, Mustian, Fowler, Kortering, & Kohler, 2009; White & Weiner, 2004)
- Better-quality Individualized Education Programs (IEPs) (Hunt & Farron-Davis, 1992)
- Fewer absences from school and referrals for disruptive behavior (Helmstetter, Curry, Brennan, & Sampson-Saul, 1998)
- Achievement of more IEP goals (Brinker & Thorpe, 1984; Idol, 2006)

Some researchers have also found a correlation between inclusive placement of students with disabilities and positive outcomes for students without disabilities, including significantly greater progress in reading and math when all students are taught in inclusive settings (Cole, Waldron, & Majd, 2004) and increased assignment completion and classroom participation when students without disabilities provided peer support to students with disabilities (Cushing & Kennedy, 1997). Kalambouka, Farrell, and Dyson's (2007) meta-analysis of inclusive education research found 81 percent of the reported outcomes showed including students with disabilities resulted in either positive or neutral effects for students without disabilities. Similarly, in their recent randomized control experiment, Fruth and Woods (2015) found no significant difference in the reading, science, or social studies performance of students without disabilities in inclusive classes and concluded, "Stakeholders ought to take an unwavering stance toward including students with disabilities into the general education classroom" (p. 360).

So, despite the original intent of the federal special education law favoring placement in general education and a growing body of research showing clear benefits for educating students with and without disabilities in general education classes with supplemental aids and services, why are thousands of students, particularly those with intellectual disability, still spending most of their day in separate classes or educational settings far from their neighborhood schools? According to *The Condition of Education 2013*, 6.4 million children and youth ages 3–21 received special education services in 2010–2011, or about 13 percent of all public school students (Aud, Wilkinson-Flicker, Kristapovich, Rathbun, Wang, & Zhang, 2013). Seven percent of these students are labelled with intellectual disability, six percent with autism, and two percent with multiple disabilities, totaling 960,000 students; the majority of students with these labels are segregated from their peers without disabilities and are at risk for poor educational outcomes due, in part, to their placement outside of the general education classrooms for the majority of their school day. We suggest the persistent segregation of these subgroups of students with intellectual disabilities is due in large part to the inherent flaws of the LRE mandate, not just in a lack of understanding of the mandate or in prejudice towards students with intellectual disability.

4   Flaws in the Principles Underlying the LRE Mandate

There are six flaws in the principles underlying the LRE mandate representing philosophical, conceptual, and implementation elements. The first flaw is that not every student shares the same freedoms or rights; certain students with disabilities are disproportionately segregated from their peers without disabilities without impunity. *PARC v. Commonwealth of Pennsylvania* (1972) attorney Thomas Gilhool explains the legal origin of the least restrictive concept based on the principle of freedom of speech:

> Least restrictive environment came from that run of cases that was about improving the institution and it came from a longer tradition of free speech cases where when you were doing anything that touched on free speech, you had to choose the way of doing it that was least restrictive of free speech. It was not from the quality side of the Constitution, but from the due process side of the Constitution. (Gilhool, 2011, p. 16)

Gilhool's explanation provides a view of LRE that is based in our constitutional civil rights. Rather than allowing for justification to remove some children from particular contexts and place them in more restrictive ones for their own good, Gilhool suggests we think in terms of how the LRE interpretations have been used to limit students' freedoms. Gilhool points out that the LRE changed the focus from quality of education to due process rights, thus legitimizing segregation as acceptable for some students. His point begs us to ask the question: Would the outcome be different three decades hence if the *quality of educational services and outcomes* rather than *placement* were the focus?

In practice LRE asks educational teams not to determine how integrated students should be but rather to what degree they should be segregated (Taylor, 1988). It is based on the premise that students with disabilities have to earn the right to move from more to less restrictive settings through improvements in their performance. For students with intellectual disability whose progress is sometimes slow, they may never meet the criteria for moving out of a segregated setting (Taylor, 1988).

The LRE mandate as educational policy is inextricably linked to cultural beliefs about disability that have been termed by some as ableism; that is "the devaluation of disability" that "results in societal attitudes that uncritically assert that it is better for a child to walk than roll, speak than sign, read print than Braille, spell independently than use a spell-check, and hang out with nondisabled kids as opposed to other disabled kids" (Hehir, 2002, p. 1). This is the second flaw in the LRE mandate. Jordan (2005) explains further:

> Attributions of disability deflect attention from the ways in which these students are marginalized by constructions of normalcy that privilege the white, middle- and upper middle-class, able-bodied male. These constructions often reflect the tacit norms and assumptions of those from ... the "culture of power" .... Abnormality then comes to be defined as the extent to which certain lifestyles and behaviors vary from the mainstream, and the construct of disability is made available to support a medical orientation and response toward these differences. (pp. 130–131)

This indictment of LRE as the impetus for creating bureaucratic (and separate) general and special education systems perpetuates educational and social inequalities. Beratan (2008) interpreted the LRE clause "to the maximum extent appropriate," as implying "to the maximum extent appropriate to an individual's deficit" (p. 3). He argued that this implication of an inherently separate system is one way that IDEA and its LRE mandate exemplifies a message of ableism within the educational system. A process in which the individual is implicated as having a problem frees the system itself from critique:

> Although the original impetus for the creation of special education was to serve a neglected population, in reality special education's separate location perpetuated the mainstream education system's refusal to work with a wider range of human abilities. The rights and ethics discourse states that the existence of a dual educational system prevents systemic changes to make education responsive to an increasingly diverse society .... The existence of parallel educational systems privileges professional groups (e.g., school psychologists, special educators, etc.) that control specific areas of expertise, which in turn affords them privileged positions and compels them to resist inclusion efforts. (Artiles, Harris-Murri, & Rostenburg, 2006, p. 261)

Furthermore, these parallel educational systems in which students are sorted by presumed performance hierarchies perpetuate negative stereotypes of certain students with disabilities compared to their typically developing peers (Siperstein, Parker, Bardon, & Widaman, 2007). The value ascribed to difference is a key point, whether that difference is about ability or other social attributes. Similarly, where Moll, Amanti, Neff, and Gonzalez (1992) argued that teachers should look to ethnic minorities' "funds of knowledge" rather than using a deficit model for literacy instruction, in a model that views disability as diversity (rather than tragedy, deviance, or deficit), teachers and policy makers refocus educational efforts on ways of knowing students with disabilities as contributing members of society (Lawrence-Brown & Sapon-Shevin, 2013). While the idea of identifying and utilizing the positive attributes of a student with disabilities is not new (Gartner & Lipsky, 1987; Wansart, 1995), it seems to have been relegated to the sidelines in large part because the practices of special education are bound by policies influenced by the LRE mandate.

The third flaw in the LRE mandate is evident in the prejudicial treatment of students with the intellectual disability label. How we define intelligence is culturally bound (Gould, 1991; Trent, 1994) and plays a role in the interpretation of the LRE mandate. Individualized Education Program (IEP) team members determine placement and justify more restrictive settings when students are identified with an intellectual disability. Intellectual shortcomings in particular have been ascribed not only to certain individuals with disabilities, but to other marginalized groups including African-Americans. Kliewer, Biklen, and Kasa-Hendrickson (2006) posit that the explanation for the determination of intellectual disability "may be less a biologically based actuality and much more akin to social impositions historically ascribed to children outside the circles of educational privilege" (p. 168). The continuous debates about intellectual quotient and race (Beratan, 2008; Borthwick, 2010) and the successful argument for changing the term mental retardation to intellectual disability provide examples of the troubling subjectivity and sociocultural and historical influences on the concept of intelligence (Harris, 2013).

In addition to the influence of individual and broader societal beliefs about disability, the interpretations of and decisions about LRE are based on historical precedents in local schools, how teachers have been prepared, and the strength of parent advocacy and privilege (Biklen, 1982; IDEA, 2004, p. 118 STAT. 2649, (4); Nisbet, 2004; Sauer & Albanesi, 2013). These idiosyncratic understandings and decision-making processes constitute the fourth flaw in the LRE mandate and they result in vast discrepancies in placement data depending on a student's residence (Hehir et al., 2012; LeRoy & Kulik, 2004; Parrish, 2011). Perpetuating the state-to-state variability in placement of students with a common label such as intellectual disability, the U.S. Department of Education allows *no change* in LRE as an acceptable State Performance Plan target in states that have a long history of educating students with disabilities in restrictive placements (Marks, Kurth, & Pirtle, 2013).

The fifth flaw in the LRE mandate is evidenced in the daily practice of IEP teams when they conflate placement with the location and intensity of supports and services. Despite attempts by the U.S. Department of Education to clarify the difference between IEP team decisions about placement and supplementary aids and services (i.e., "Special education is a service, not a place"), in practice the two are often conjoined (Public Law 108-446, Section 1, p. 118). Parents are told that in order for their children to receive intensive services they must agree to a restrictive placement (*Oberti v. Board of Education of Borough of Clementon School District*, 1993).

And finally, the sixth flaw in the LRE mandate is that it discourages schools from making improvements in instruction in general education by focusing on identifying and remediating perceived deficits in students' functional performance. This practice was also supported by funding formulas which in prior years "encouraged districts to place children with disabilities in separate, segregated environments" which ostensibly were staffed with personnel uniquely qualified for teaching students with the most intensive instructional and support needs (Strieker, Salisbury, & Roach, 2001, p. 18).

When the deficiency-remediation response to disability is combined with the idea that the intensity of services is inextricably linked to more restrictive environments (i.e., "We could never provide all those services in our regular school"), the LRE mandate seems logical (albeit erroneous in our opinion). Furthermore, the LRE mandate has been used to justify why students with intellectual disability are perceived to need restrictive educational settings in order to receive the specialized services that will make them "better enough" to move to less restrictive settings. The practical result of these attitudes and beliefs (rather than research) is the perpetuation of a variety of specious arguments that are commonly made for separate educational settings for students with intellectual disabilities such as: (a) Specialized instructional practices or supplementary aids and services needed by students with disabilities cannot be implemented in a general education classroom; (b) The extent of curricular modifications needed by some students is so great that the general education curriculum it is no longer recognizable; (c) Some students need an exclusively life-skills curriculum that cannot be delivered in a general education classroom; and (d) General education teachers do not have the skills to teach some students with disabilities.

Such justifications for more restrictive educational settings impact the daily living experiences of the children and youth with intellectual disability and their families with arguably dismal long-term outcomes (Ryndak et al., 2012; Wagner, Newman, Cameto, Levine, & Garza, 2006).

5 Placement Patterns for Students with Intellectual Disability

The influence of the LRE mandate can be found in placement data reported annually by the states to the U.S. Department of Education. Despite a 30-year trend in educating more students with disabilities in general education environments, most students with intellectual disability still spend the majority of their school day in a separate class or other segregated setting. For example, from 2002–2011 the percentage of all students ages 6–21 served under IDEIA Part B inside the regular class 80 percent or more of the day increased from 48.2 to 61.1 percent. However, the average of all states' placement of students with intellectual disability at least 80 percent of the day in general education as reported in December 2014 was only 17.1 (U.S. Department of Education, 2014). In their analysis of state and national trends of placement data since 2004 using State Performance Plans and the National Center for Educational Statistics, Kurth, Morningstar, and Kozleski (2014) found students with low-incidence disabilities (including what they termed significant cognitive impairment) most often appear in the most restrictive settings, illustrating the lack of progress toward inclusion over a 10-year period.

The variability in placement data from state to state provides additional evidence for specious if not discriminatory placement decision-making that is guided by the LRE mandate. According to the 36th Annual Report to Congress on the Implementation of IDEA (U.S. Department of Education, 2014), the percent of students with intellectual disability educated at least 80 percent of the day in general education classes ranged from lows of 4.4 in Washington, 4.8 in New Jersey, and 5.5 in Nevada, to highs of 64 in Iowa, 48.6 in Puerto Rico, and 45.5 in Alabama. In their recent analysis of geographic variability in Ohio, Brock and Schaefer (2015) found students with developmental disabilities spent more time in general education classrooms if they lived outside of large urban districts. Kurth and colleagues (2014) also found geographic variability in placement patterns.

Smith and Kozleski (2005) cited a chapter within the Eleventh Annual Report to Congress on the Implementation of the Education of the Handicapped Act that stated, "Attributing meaning to the degree of variability across states may be more a matter of values than empirical analysis" (U.S. Department of Education, 1989, p. 29). Thomas Parrish (2011) from the Center on Special Education Finance put it this way: "Are the students in [a state like Washington] that different from the students in [a state like Iowa] to justify such large differences in placement patterns?"

While the relationship between placement and location variability is now recognized, responses aimed at improving inclusive placements, particularly for students with intellectual and developmental disabilities, are questionable.

For instance, although a 2011 report by the National Institute on Urban School Improvement/ LeadScape recommended that states and the federal government take ambitious steps to increase the percent of students with disabilities served in general education at least 80 percent of the day, the authors made a troubling exception for students with severe disabilities (which includes students with intellectual disability):

> Since approximately 3 percent of students need an alternative curriculum and assessment, it raises the question of whether targets for [the percent of students educated in the regular class less than 40 percent of the day] should aim to reduce service delivery in this category to [3%]. (National Institute on Urban School Improvement/LeadScape, 2011, p. 76)

Finally, in a recent study of six southwestern states, Marks, Kurth, and Pirtle (2013) found a weak relationship between LRE targets and actual changes as reflected in their State Performance Plans (SPP). Therefore, although states are required to set measurable and rigorous targets in these improvement plans, the actual changes do not support the federal government's reliance on this accountability process to increase inclusive placements for all students. These findings illustrate several problems: (a) Strong proponents of inclusion suggesting that some students—the 3 percent who "need alternate assessment and curriculum"—might never be included in general education (National Institute on Urban School Improvement, 2011, p. 76); (b) Accepting "no-improvement" as a legitimate SPP target; (c) Slippage in the percentage of time students spend in general education reported by some states; and (d) Students with intellectual disability and/or students of color being the most segregated within minimal improvement over time.

Placement patterns have also been shown to discriminate by race, disproportionally segregating African-American, Hispanic, and other non-White students with disabilities (Oswald, Coutinho, & Best, 2002). "In some states," write Smith and Kozleski (2005), "Black students were more than two and a half times as likely as their White peers to be identified for special education services for mental retardation" (p. 275). According to Smith and Kozleski (2005),

> The movement to include students with disabilities in general education and the continued struggle to racially integrate America's schools share similar paths. These paths diverge, however, because the progressive inclusion of students with disabilities has thus far largely involved and benefited children and families from the White middle class. (p. 271)

Sauer and Albanesi (2013) draw on sociology and disability studies to question the role of white privilege as educated parents in the decision-making process. They build on the work of other scholars who have also identified the influence of traditional power structures on identification and inclusive placement decision-making (Beratan, 2008; Brantlinger; 2003; Donovan & Cross, 2002; Ferri & Connor, 2005; Harry & Klingner, 2006; Ong-Dean, 2009). Together the *Brown* (1954) decision and the passage of the federal special education law PL 94-142 seemed a powerful force for creating schools that were inclusive of students previously marginalized due to race and/or disability. Almost 40 years of data, however, show that this goal is far from being realized. Although disproportionality in the prevalence rates of students of color with intellectual disability has been identified as a systemic problem, federal agencies and advocacy organizations have only begun to examine the issue more closely (Edwards, Blanchett, Crocker, & Ransom, 2007).

6 Seminal Court Cases Involving Least Restrictive Environment

Although the courts mandate attitudinal change, court decisions have led to systemic changes such as the *Brown* case that made clear "separate educational facilities are inherently unequal." We suggest that if the EHA had adopted such clear language, the courts would not be caught up in individual due-process cases involving LRE-related placement issues that in effect maintain barriers to inclusion. Before the passage of the Education for All Handicapped Children Act in 1975 (EHA), schools could categorically refer to children as uneducable and send them to institutions, thus denying them access to a free and appropriate public education. The current debate centers less on the educability issue and more on placement and access to the general education curriculum. Since EHA was enacted, the meaning and operationalization of LRE have been debated at every level of the education system. Rather than invoking the separate is not equal mandate and operationalizing the idea that special education is a service rather than a place as stipulated in the latest reauthorization of the law, IDEA still requires that schools make available a continuum of placement options ranging from the general education classroom to residential and hospital settings.

The vagueness of the law and disagreements about appropriate learning environments for students with intellectual disability have led both parents and schools to ask courts to mediate these disputes. These cases are often multi-faceted, addressing issues such as students' ability to benefit, adequate provision of supplementary aids and services, unreasonable burden on staff or resources, impact on other students, system-wide discrimination towards a sub-category/class of students with disabilities, or procedural violations. At times parents or guardians have argued for placement in the general education classroom in the neighborhood school, believing it to be the least restrictive setting (*Beth B. v. Van Clay*, 2002; *Lessard v. Wilton-Lyndeborough Cooperative School, NH*, 2010). In other cases the school districts made this argument (*K. B. v. Nebo School District*, 2004; *Walszak v. Florida*, 1998), but many such cases involve years of appeal and reversals of decisions involving LRE decisions.

One of the most important LRE decisions was made in the case of *Oberti v. Board of Education of Borough of Clementon School District* (1993), in which the school district was deemed negligent in their efforts to provide the student with the necessary supports resulting in his "unsuccessful placement." Schools were told they could not justify more restrictive placements simply because a teacher did not know how to teach the child. This decision had a direct impact on what can be justified as least restrictive. This case is also notable because the federal judge who decided the case opined that "Inclusion is a right, not a privilege for a select few" (Kluth, Villa, & Thousand, 2001, p. 25).

In the *Board of Education of Hendrick Hudson Central School District v. Amy Rowley* case (1982), the courts disagreed on the level of services needed to support a student in an inclusive setting. The case went all the way to the Supreme Court, establishing a basic level for opportunity indicating adequate services need only be provided to a student, not those providing maximum benefit. This decision might then lead some parents or other members of educational teams to advocate for placing a student in a more restrictive setting (e.g., a school for deaf children) where services such as an interpreter might be automatic, thus avoiding a debate about what constitutes adequate versus maximum.

In *Sacramento City Unified District v. Holland* (1994), the school district's justification for a more restrictive educational setting was not upheld. The ruling cited the evidence based on Rachel Holland's general education teacher, who testified that Rachel's behavior was not disruptive nor a distraction, and that her IEP goals could be addressed in the general education classroom with some curricular modifications and support services. In this case the Ninth Circuit (primarily composed of Western states) referred to the school district's own "four-factor test," which included educational and non-academic benefits, the effect of the child's presence on the teacher and other children, and the cost (Gallegos, 2010, p. 11).

The proximity of the educational placement to the child's home has also been disputed. Whereas the court in *Oberti* (1993) held a preference for a child to be taught in his neighborhood school, other courts disagreed (*Murray v. Montrose County*, 1995). In the *Murray* case the parents argued legislative history set the LRE precedence for local school placement. However, the court quoted the statute as saying "... nothing about where, within a school district, that inclusion shall take place" (Gallegos, 2010, p. 19), thus justifying busing Tyler Murray 10 miles from his home to attend a different school that offered special services targeting services for students with significant disabilities rather than his neighborhood school. In *Roncker v. Walter* (1983), it was decided to remove Neill Roncker from a school where he "had contact with nondisabled students" to "an entirely segregated county school" (Gallegos, 2010, p. 4). The LRE justification in the case focused on comparing the academic opportunities between these contexts, successfully arguing that the more segregated placement was superior (Gallegos, 2010). In such cases segregated schools were argued to be the least restrictive.

The last category of LRE disputes concerns non-compliance with the required process of determining a child's educational placement. In several settlements parents won reimbursement for private school placements, often resulting from procedural violations (see *LM v. Capistrano Unified School*, 2009; *Howard S. v. Friendswood Independent School District*). In other cases entire school districts or states have been found to have systemic LRE abuses (Hehir et al., 2012; *Jamie S. v. Milwaukee Public Schools*, 2001). A 1993 class action lawsuit in Connecticut (*P. J. et al. v. State of Connecticut, Board of Education*), settled in May 2002, outlined a series of expected outcomes, including an increase in the percent of students with intellectual disability to be placed in regular classes, as well as an increase in the mean and median percent of the school day that students with intellectual disability spend with nondisabled students in the school they would attend if not disabled. In the 2005 settlement for the *Gaskin v. Pennsylvania* class action lawsuit filed in 1994, a Special Education Advisory Panel on LRE was set up specifically to address restrictive placement complaints after lawyers successfully argued that supplementary aids and services were not provided to students (Public Interest Law Center of Philadelphia, 2013). These settlements offered specific goals and supports to enact the changes that the courts deemed necessary to comply with their ruling. Similarly, in a review of special education across the state of Massachusetts, Hehir et al. (2012) found "an uneven picture of special education policy and practice" (p. 2), where low-income students and students of color were disproportionately served in more restrictive settings and that these placements may have contributed to their lower performance on standardized tests. In their subsequent analysis, Hehir, Schifter, Grindal, Ng, & Eidelman (2014) recommended "the State should actively intervene in districts that fail to provide effective inclusive options for students with disabilities" (p. 19).

The aforementioned and other LRE cases serve to support our argument that the LRE mandate—both its conceptual underpinnings and the inconsistent way it is implemented—is irreparably flawed. Specialized services and programming are often concentrated in certain schools within a school district, thus creating cluster-type programs that result in a disproportionate number of students with particular disabilities in one school. This puts parents in a difficult situation: in order to get the services their child needs, they believe that they must accept a more restrictive placement than their child's home school. This leads us back to the problem we find with sanctioning separate placements in which large groups of students with intellectual disability have been denied not just access to general education opportunities but quality educational services broadly (Causton-Theoharis, Theoharis, Orsati, & Cosier, 2011).

Although the court judgments in favor of inclusive educational placements have helped individual students, scholars have argued that the individual rights-based legal system has a limited ability to create systemic change. Effecting such changes are neither within the court's purview nor an effective way to influence large-scale changes in policy and practice to benefit an entire population of students with the intellectual disability label (Beratan, 2008; Palley, 2006; Skilton-Sylvester & Slesaransky-Poe, 2009; Zuna & Turnbull, 2004). Skilton-Sylvester and Slesaransky-Poe (2009) noted that legal mandates under IDEA focused exclusively on the rights of a few without ever addressing the normative assumptions that exist in schools and classrooms in ways that could change the system for all students. Schools then take their cues from individual case-law interpretations, which may ultimately be more limiting than liberating (Beratan, 2008; Palley, 2006; Zuna & Turnbull, 2004):

> As a result of the different standards that are used by federal circuit courts, the extent to which courts show a preference toward including children with disabilities with their nondisabled peers varies greatly. Much of this variation can be traced to the facts of the cases that the circuit courts reviewed. As a result of the differing standards, the extent to which school districts and states have facilitated the inclusion of students with disabilities varies greatly. Moreover, because none of these cases were class actions, the decisions will not necessarily lead to structural changes in the overall system but rather to improvements in the rights of individual children in a system not necessarily set up to include them in the LRE. As a result, other children will likely continue to be excluded and to fall through the cracks that remain. (Palley, 2006, p. 232)

Even when class-action cases related to LRE in Connecticut, New Jersey, and Pennsylvania were decided in favor of more inclusive placements for students with disabilities, the percent of students with intellectual disability in these states spending 80 percent or more of their time in general education still remains unacceptably low at 43.7, 4.8, and 12.4 percent respectively (U.S. Department of Education, 2014).

Bringing more due process or class-action lawsuits burdens parents and advocacy organizations with proving that students with intellectual disability deserve the right to learn alongside their same-age classmates and continues to situate the problem within individual students rather than within the non-adaptive educational systems within which they are schooled:

> Similar to institutional racism, institutional ableism is distinguished from the individual bigotry toward people with disabilities by the existence of systemic, pervasive, and habitual policies and practices that disadvantage individuals based on their abilities. But because of institutional ableism's hold on our society, it is unlikely that any legal remedy will eliminate the educational inequity faced by students with disabilities. (Fierros, 2006, p. 2)

Individual or class-action lawsuits are inadequate because if they are brought against school districts or states, changes will occur for only a very few—those with privileged cultural capital based on income, class, and color—and any positive results will take many years. Witness the time that it took for Connecticut's P. J. case to be settled (2002) compared to when it was originally brought to the court (1991). While illustrating how LRE is typically interpreted by the courts in the District of Columbia as "least restrictive environment available" rather than "least restrictive environment needed," Carson (2015) explained how LRE deprives many students from integrated educational experiences. While such legal suggestions to fix LRE might be useful in a court of law, we find this solution does not address the underlying issues of institutional ableism that Fierros (2006) and others have brought to light (Beratan, 2008; Brantlinger; 2003; Donovan & Cross, 2002; Ferri & Connor, 2005; Harry & Klingner, 2006; Ong-Dean, 2009).

7 Reforms to Address the Flaws in the Least Restrictive Environment Mandate

The central thesis of this chapter is that there are intractable flaws inherent in the principles underlying the LRE mandate (not simply problems with implementation or accountability) that create barriers to the education of students with intellectual disability in general education classrooms and their enjoyment of the benefits that such placement bestows. We echo the recommendations of others who have called for the creation of a unified system of general education in which all students are general education students and all federal, state, and local educational resources support both equity and excellence for all students (Gartner & Lipsky, 1987; King, Capullo, Kozleski, & Gonzales, 2009). In a universal general education system an LRE mandate based on the current continuum would be unnecessary because all students would be educated in general education classrooms.

Elements of such a universal general education system are being piloted in several states through the SWIFT project, funded by the U.S. Department of Education Office of Special Education programs. The SWIFT educational model—SchoolWide Integrated Framework for Transformation—builds school capacity to provide academic and behavioral support to improve outcomes for all students through equity-based inclusion. In schools implementing the model there is a focus on broad and deep restructuring of general education, special education, and other entitlement-based supports and services. By addressing multiple features of policy and practice within five broad domains—administrative leadership; multi-tiered systems of support; an integrated educational framework; inclusive policy, structure, and practice; and family and community engagement—SWIFT aims to improve outcomes for all students within inclusive contexts (SWIFT, 2015, p. 2). This project is providing technical assistance to 18 school districts in five states to help them create sustainable systems, policies, and practices that use all of their resources to implement multi-tiered systems of supports (MTSS) within universally designed curriculum and instruction (UDL). The directors of this project are not calling for new legislation and believe that

> ... the debate regarding whether or not separate educational systems are effective should be put aside in favor of allocation of all resources available for the benefit of all students. Through a MTSS framework each student is given, based on their measured educational need, what they instructionally need to succeed when they need it, rendering irrelevant the physical location of supports and services (i.e., special education is a service, not a place). (Sailor & McCart, 2014, p. 58)

We wonder what will happen, though, to the students in the other approximately 132,000 schools in 13,000 districts in the U.S. not participating in the SWIFT effort that are still governed by the flawed LRE mandate. How long will the children and their families have to wait for the SWIFT effort to expand? Will the outcomes of the SWIFT project be so compelling as to influence future reauthorizations of the Every Student Succeeds Act (ESSA) (2015) and the Individuals With Disabilities Education Act (2004) so that the current construction of LRE shifts to a policy where the appropriate placement for all students is the general education classroom?

Although we acknowledge the limitations of legislation, it is a worthwhile discussion to consider what we have at our disposal to enact change. We propose a more radical transformation where a universal general education law encompasses educational policy and practice for all students, and where the Americans With Disabilities Act (ADA) can be used to change our legal focus from due process to freedom (Gilhool, 2011). The ADA clearly prohibits segregation of people with disabilities. In the *Olmstead v. L. C.* (1999) decision in which the plaintiffs sought "freedom from undue restraint," the court cited the ADA's integration mandate, writing that institutions are "a form of discrimination based on disability—discrimination that perpetuates unwarranted assumptions about their capabilities and their worthiness" (Bazelon Center for Mental Health Law, 2016, para. 4). In the U.S. Department of Justice's recent investigation of Georgia, they found the use of a statewide segregated program to deliver special education and related services violated ADA "by unnecessarily segregating students with disabilities from their peers" (U.S. Department of Justice, 2015, p. 1). Interviews with administrators in general education schools said the state did not provide the support services nor the training teachers needed to enable successful inclusive education. The report also indicated students were often "stuck" in segregated programs by exit criteria with higher standards than those expected of typically developing peers. Because the specialized program exists, the report explains, the state relied on it to serve students, providing evidence to support our argument that because it exits, it needed to be filled with students. Arguably, the ADA is a more powerful, all-encompassing tool than IDEA.

We are not recommending that students with disabilities be treated exactly like students without disabilities, despite Palley's (2006) recommendation that a unified system of education for all students not include the identification of students with disabilities as a special class. We believe that several groups of students who currently show the poorest educational outcomes—students living in poverty, minority students, English language learners, and students with the most significant disabilities—are entitled to a unique status as a special class in a universal general education system until their access to research-based instruction and their school and post-school outcomes approach those of their non-marginalized classmates. These rights could be protected by incorporating into a new universal general education law accountability measures for these subgroups coupled with oversight from the U.S. Department of

Education and the Department of Justice. We believe that a merger of IDEA and ESSA would only be acceptable for parents of students with disabilities and their advocates if most of the same rights afforded to students and families in IDEA were maintained.

This new universal general education law would have an increased emphasis on specific evidence-based practices that have shown to be effective for students with and without disabilities, such as Universal Design for Learning; multi-tiered systems of academic and behavioral support; positive behavior interventions and supports; the use of technology to promote accessibility to instruction and provide multiple options for students to show what they know; self-determination; balanced literacy approaches; and assistive technology, including augmentative and alternative communication.

In this reformed educational system all federal, state, and local resources would be dedicated to creating inclusive school systems rather than on maintaining the current separate systems of education on the restrictive end of the continuum that draw millions of dollars in resources away from local schools. Imagine if the resources spent on special education and special schools (infrastructure, administration and staff, materials, and transportation) were available to the public schools to meet all children's needs in inclusive contexts. For example, a 2007 report from the New Jersey School Board Association (NJSBA) found that special education services cost over $3.3 billion dollars a year, with a significant proportion of funds spent on out-of-district private special education schools and transportation. According to the NJSBA, out-of-district placements involve 10 percent of New Jersey's special education population, but make up 40 percent of the total cost of special education (Molenaar & Luciano, 2007).

Another important element of a unified educational system would be a unified system of teacher, administrator, and related service personnel preparation at the pre-service level. Many universities already have dual certification programs in general and special education at the preschool and elementary education levels (e.g., Syracuse University's Inclusive Elementary and Special Education Program).

8   Conclusion

The U.S. has a history of unequal treatment in that "people with disabilities, as a group, occupy an inferior status in our society, and are severely disadvantaged socially, vocationally, economically, and educationally" (42 U.S.C. 12101 (a)(6)). Forty years after he served as lawyer for the plaintiffs in *Brown v. Board of Education of Topeka* (1954), Supreme Court Justice Thurgood Marshall drew parallels between the civil and disability rights movements when giving an opinion in *City of Cleburne v. Cleburne Living Center, Inc.* (1985):

> The mentally retarded have been subject to a lengthy and tragic history of segregation and discrimination that can only be called grotesque, fueled by the rising tide of social Darwinism, the "science" of eugenics, the xenophobia of those years. Leading medical authorities and others began to portray the feebleminded as a menace to society and civilization responsible in large degree for many if not all of our social problems. A regime of state-mandated segregation and degradation soon emerged that in its virulent and bigotry rivaled, and indeed paralleled the worst excesses of Jim Crow ... Retarded children were categorically excluded from public schools based on the false stereotype that all were uneducable, and on the purported need to protect non-retarded children from them. State laws deemed the retarded unfit for citizenship. (p. 16)

Another 30 years later, we find it troubling that our profession continues to question the efficacy of inclusion, often using the LRE mandate as an argument for restricting a student's freedom to benefit from a general education experience. Although some individuals with intellectual disability and their advocates have managed to negotiate the current system to their benefit, LRE has been used to perpetuate segregation. It is our hope that by acknowledging the intractable flaws of the LRE mandate Taylor (1988) identified decades ago, we might encourage our colleagues to redirect their attention away from piecemeal efforts to fix these flaws and instead focus on designing new laws, policies, and practices that are inclusive of all students, including those with intellectual disability. Although we will continue to collaborate with educational professionals and families to develop inclusive supports and services for children with intellectual disability on a case-by-case basis, we would prefer to work within a universally designed general education system that supports the structural changes our society must make to move forward in a thoughtful way because we cannot stand by while another generation of students with intellectual disability are segregated.

Acknowledgment

This chapter originally appeared as: Sauer, J. S., & Jorgensen, C. M. (2016). Still caught in the continuum: A critical analysis of least restrictive environment and its effect on placement of students with intellectual disability. *Inclusion*, 4(2), 56–74. Reprinted here with permission.

References

Americans With Disabilities Act of 1990 ("ADA"), 42 U.S.C. §§ 12101-12213.

Artiles, A. J., Harris-Murri, N., & Rostenburg, D. (2006). Inclusion as social justice: Critical notes on discourses, assumptions, and the road ahead. *Theory into Practice, 45*(3), 260–268.

Aud, S., Wilkinson-Flicker, S., Kristapovich, P., Rathbun, A., Wang, X., & Zhang, J. (2013). *The condition of education 2013* (NCES 2013-037). U.S. Department of Education, National Center for Education Statistics. http://nces.ed.gov/pubsearch

Bazelon Center for Mental Health Law. (2016). *The Olmstead Decision.* http://www.bazelon.org/Where-We-Stand/Community-Integration/Olmstead-Implementing-the-Integration-Mandate/The-Olmstead-Decision-.aspx

Beratan, G. D. (2008). The song remains the same: Transposition and the disproportionate representation of minority students in special education. *Race, Ethnicity, and Education, 11*(4), 337–354. doi:10.1080/13613320802478820

Beth B. v. Van Clay, 282 F.3d. 493 (7th Cir. 2002).

Biklen, D. (1982). The least restrictive environment: Its application to education. *Child & Youth Services, 5*(1–2), 121–144.

Board of Education v. Rowley, 458 U.S. 176 (1982).

Borthwick, C. (2010). Racism, IQ, and down's syndrome. *Disability & Society, 11*(3), 403–410. doi:10.1080/09687599627688

Brantlinger, E. (2003). *Dividing classes: How the middle class negotiates and rationalizes school advantage.* Routledge Falmer.

Brinker, R. P., & Thorpe, M. E. (1984). Integration of intellectually handicapped students and the proportion of IEP objectives achieved. *Exceptional Children, 51*, 168–175.

Brock, M. E., & Schaefer, J. M. (2015). Location matters: Geographic location and educational placement of students with developmental disabilities. *Research and Practice for Persons with Severe Disabilities, 40*(2), 154–164. doi:10.1177/1540796915591988

Brown v. Board of Education of Topeka, 347 U.S. 483. (1954).

Carson, C. (2015, June). Rethinking special education's "least restrictive environment" requirement. *Michigan Law Review, 113*(8), 1397–1426.

Causton-Theoharis, J., Theoharis, G., Orsati, F., & Cosier, M. (2011). Does self-contained special education deliver on its promises? A critical inquiry into research and practice. *Journal of Special Education Leadership, 24*(2), 61–78.

City of Cleburne v. Cleburne Living Center, Inc., 473 U.S. 432, 105 S. Ct. 3249, 87 L. Ed. 2d 313, 1985 U.S.

Cole, C. M., Waldron, N., & Majd, M. (2004). Academic progress of students across inclusive and traditional settings. *Mental Retardation, 42*, 136–144.

Cosier, M., Causton-Theoharis, J., & Theoharis, G. (2013). Does access matter? Time in general education and achievement for students with disabilities. *Remedial and Special Education, 34*(6), 323–332.

Cushing, L. S., & Kennedy, C. H. (1997). Academic effects of providing peer support in general education classrooms on students without disabilities. *Journal of Applied Behavior Analysis, 30*, 139–151.

Danforth, S., & Naraian, S. (2015). This new field of inclusive education: Beginning a dialogue on conceptual foundations. *Intellectual and Developmental Disabilities, 53*(1), 70–85. doi:10.1352/1934-9556-53.1.70

Dessemontet, R. S., Bless, G., & Morin, D. (2012). Effects of inclusion on the academic achievement and adaptive behaviour of children with intellectual disabilities. *Journal of Intellectual Disability Research, 56*(6), 579–587.

Education for All Handicapped Children Act of 1975, 20 U.S.C. §1401. Federal Register, August 23, 1977, p. 42497.

Edwards, R., Blanchett, B., Crocker, A., & Ransom, B. (2007, December). *People of color with significant disabilities and their families: Prevalence, challenges, and successes.* Paper presented at the TASH Conference.

Every Student Succeeds Act. P.L. 114-95. (2015).

Ferguson, D. L. (2008). International trends in inclusive education: The continuing challenge to teach each and every one. *International Journal of Special Needs Education, 23*, 109–120. doi:10.1080/08856250801946236

Ferri, B., & Connor, D. (2005). Tools of exclusion: Race, disability, and (re)segregated education. *Teachers College Record, 107*(3), 453–474.

Fierros, E. G. (2006). One size does not fit all: A response to institutionalizing inequity. *Disability Studies Quarterly, 26*(2).

Fisher, M., & Meyer, L. (2002). Development and social competence after two years for students enrolled in inclusive and self-contained educational programs. *Research and Practice for Persons with Intellectual Disabilities, 27*, 165–174.

Fruth, J. D., & Woods, M. N. (2015). Academic performance of students without disabilities in the inclusive environment. *Education, 135*(3), 351–361.

Gallegos, E. M. (2010). *Least restrictive environment.* Walsh, Anderson, Brown, Gallegos, and Green, P.C. http://www.bie.edu/

Gartner, A., & Lipsky, D. (1987). Beyond special education: Toward a quality system for all students. *Harvard Educational Review, 57*(4), 367–396.

Gaskin v. Pennsylvania, 389 F. Supp. 2d 628, 644 (E.D. Pa. 2005).

Gilhool, T. K. (2011). *Right to education* [Interview transcript]. Interview by L. Sonnenborn. Visionary Voices Project. Temple University. http://disabilities.temple.edu/voices/detailVideo.asp?mediaCode=006-01

Gould, S. J. (1996). *The mismeasure of man* (rev. ed.). W.W. Norton and Company.

Guralnick, M. J., Connor, R., Hammond, M., Gottman, J. M., & Kinnish, K. (1996). Immediate effects of mainstreamed settings on the social interactions and social integration of preschool children. *American Journal on Mental Retardation, 100*, 359–377.

Harris, J. C. (2013). New terminology for mental retardation in DSM-5 and ICD-11. *Current Opinion Psychiatry, 26*(3), 260–262. http://www.medscape.com/viewarticle/782769

Harry, B., & Klingner, J. K. (2006). *Why are so many minority students in special education? Understanding race and disability in schools.* Teachers College Press.

Hehir, T. (2002). Eliminating ableism in education. *Harvard Educational Review, 72*(1), 1–32.

Hehir, T., Grindal, T., & Eidelman, H. (2012). *Review of special education in the commonwealth of Massachusetts.* Massachusetts Department of Elementary and Secondary Education.

Hehir, T., Schifter, L., Grindal, T., Ng, M., & Eidelman, H. (2014). *Review of special education in the commonwealth of Massachusetts: A synthesis report.* Massachusetts Department of Elementary and Secondary Education.

Helmstetter, E., Curry, C. A., Brennan, M., & Sampson-Saul, M. (1998). Comparison of general and special education classrooms of students with intellectual disabilities. *Education and Training in Mental Retardation and Developmental Disabilities, 33,* 216–227.

Howard S. v. Friendswood Independent School District, 454 F. Supp. 634. (1978).

Hunt, P., & Farron-Davis, F. (1992). A preliminary investigation of IEP quality and content associated with placement in general education versus special education classes. *Journal of the Association for Persons with Intellectual Handicaps, 17,* 247–253.

Hunt, P., Farron-Davis, F., Beckstead, S., Curtis, D., & Goetz, L. (1994). Evaluating the effects of placement of students with intellectual disabilities in general education versus special classes. *Journal of the Association for Persons with Intellectual Handicaps, 19,* 200–214.

Idol, L. (2006). Toward inclusion of special education students in general education: A program evaluation of eight schools. *Remedial and Special Education, 27*(2), 77–94.

Inclusion: The pros and cons. *Issues ... About Change, 4*(3). http://www.sedl.org/change/issues/issues43.html

Individuals With Disabilities Education Act, PL 105-17, 20 U.S.C. § 1400 *et seq.* (1997).

Individuals With Disabilities Education Improvement Act, PL108-446, 20 U.S.C. §1400 *et seq.* (2004).

Jackson, L. B., Ryndak, D. L., & Wehmeyer, M. L. (2008–2009). The dynamic relationship between context, curriculum, and student learning: A case for inclusive education as a research-based practice. *Research & Practice for Persons with Severe Disabilities, 33–4* (4–1), 175–195.

Jaime S. v. Milwaukee Public Schools. (2001). Case No. 01-C-928. http://www.wrightslaw.com/law/caselaw/07/WI.jamie.milwaukee.pdf

Jorgensen, C. M., McSheehan, M., & Sonnenmeier, R. M. (2007). Presumed competence reflected in the educational programs of students with IDD before and after the beyond access professional development intervention. *Journal of Intellectual and Developmental Disabilities, 32*(4), 248–262.

Jorgensen, C. M., McSheehan, M., & Sonnenmeier, R. M. (2010). *The beyond access model: Promoting membership, participation, and learning for students in the general education classroom.* Paul H. Brookes.

Kalambouka, A., Farrell, P., & Dyson, A. (2007). The impact of placing pupils with special educational needs in mainstream schools on the achievement of their peers. *Educational Research, 49*(4), 365–382.

King, K. A., Capullo, K., Kozleski, E. B., & Gonzales, J. (2009). *Inclusive education for equity* (Professional Learning for Equity Module series). The Equity Alliance at ASU.

Kliewer, C., Biklen, D., & Kasa-Hendrickson, C. (2006). Who may be literate? Disability and resistance to the cultural denial of competence. *American Educational Research Journal, 43*, 163–192.

Kluth, P., Villa, R. A., & Thousand, J. S. (2001). "Our school doesn't offer inclusion" and other legal blunders. *Educational Leadership, 59*(4), 24–27.

Kurth, J., & Mastergeorge, A. M. (2010). Academic and cognitive profiles of students with autism: Implications for classroom practice and placement. *International Journal of Special Education, 25*(2), 8–14.

Kurth, J., Morningstar, M., & Kozleski, E. B. (2014). The persistence of highly restrictive special education placements for students with low-incidence disabilities. *Research and Practice for Persons with Severe Disabilities, 39*(3), 227–239. doi:10.1177/1540796914555580

K. B. v. Nebo Sch. Dist., 379 F.3d 966 (10th Cir. 2004).

Lawrence-Brown, D., & Sapon-Shevin, M. (Eds.). (2013). *Condition critical: Key principles for equitable and inclusive education*. Teachers College Press.

LeRoy, B., & Kulik, N. (2004). *The demographics of inclusion*. Final report materials for U.S. Department of Education Office of Special Education Program Grant. Wayne State University.

Lessard v. Wilton-Lyndeborough Coop. Sch. Dist., 518 F.3d 18 (1st Cir. 2008, 08-2244 2010).

LM v. Capistrano Unified School, 556 F. 3d 900 Court of Appeals (9th Cir. 2009).

Marks, S., Kurth, J., & Pirtle, J. (2013). The effect of "measurable and rigorous" state performance goals for addressing "free and appropriate public education within the least restrictive environment." *Inclusion, 1*(3), 209–217.

Martin, E. W., Martin, R., & Treman, D. L. (1996). The legislative and litigation history of special education. *Future Child, 6*(1), 25–39.

Massachusetts Department of Education. (2014). *IEP forms.* http://www.doe.mass.edu/sped/iep/forms/pdf/PL2_6-21.pdf

McSheehan, M., Sonnenmeier, R. M., & Jorgensen, C. M. (2009). Membership, participation, and learning in general education classrooms for students with autism spectrum disorders who use AAC. In P. Mirenda & T. Iacono (Eds.), *Autism spectrum disorders and AAC* (pp. 413–442). Paul H. Brookes.

Mills v. Board of Education, 348 F. Supp. 866 (D.D.C. 1972).

Molenaar, M., & Luciano, M. (2007). *Financing special education in New Jersey*. New Jersey School Boards Association. https://www.njsba.org/specialeducation/final-report.pdf

Moll, L., Amanti, C., Neff, D., & Gonzalez, N. (1992). Funds of knowledge for teaching: Using a qualitative approach to connect homes and classrooms. *Theory into Practice, 31*(2), 132–141.

Murray v. Montrose County, 51 F.3d 921 (10th Cir. 1995).

National Institute on Urban School Improvement/LeadScape. (2011). *Indicator 5A, B, C.* http://www.directionservice.org/cadre/pdf/original_Part_B_SPPAPR_Final_8.23.11.pdf

National Research Council. (2002). *Minority students in special and gifted education* (Committee on Minority Representation in Special Education, M. S. Donovan & C. T. Cross, Eds.). Division of Behavioral and Social Sciences and Education. National Academy Press.

Nisbet, J. (2004). Commentary: Caught in the continuum. *Research & Practice for Persons with Intellectual Disabilities, 29*(4), 231–236.

Oberti v. Board of Education, 995 F.2d 1204. (1993).

Olmstead v. L.C. 527 U.S. 581. (1999).

Ong-Dean, C. (2009). *Distinguishing disability: Parents, privilege, and special education.* University of Chicago Press.

Oswald, D. P., Coutinho, M. J., & Best, A. M. (2002). Community and school predictors of overrepresentation of minority children in special education. In D. Losen & G. Orfield (Eds.), *Racial inequity in special education* (pp. 15–38). Harvard Education Press.

Palley, E. (2006). Challenges of rights-based law. *Journal of Disability Policy Studies, 16*(4), 229–235.

Parrish, T. (2011, March). *Special education funding in New Hampshire with illustrations related to adequacy, equity, and efficiency.* Presentation at the Special Education Finance Conference sponsored by the Institute on Disability, University of New Hampshire.

Pennsylvania Association for Retarded Children (PARC) v. Commonwealth of Pennsylvania, 343 F. Supp. 279. (1972).

P.J. et al. v. State of Connecticut, Board of Education. (2002). *Original* settlement filed 1993. Civic action 291CV00180 (RNC).

Public Interest Law Center of Philadelphia. (2013). *Gaskin v. Commonwealth.* http://www.pilcop.org/gaskin-v-commonwealth/

Roncker v. Walter, 700 F.2d 1058 (6th Cir.), cert. denied, 464, U.S. 864. (1983).

Ryndak, D. L., Alper, S., Ward, T., Storch, J. F., & Montgomery, J. W. (2010). Long-term outcomes of services in inclusive and self-contained settings for siblings with comparable significant disabilities. *Education and Training in Autism and Developmental Disabilities, 45,* 38–53.

Ryndak, D., Alper, S., Hughes, C., & McDonnell, J. (2012). Documenting impact of educational contexts on long-term outcomes for students with significant disabilities. *Education and Training in Autism and Developmental Disabilities, 47*(2), 127–138.

Ryndak, D. L., Morrison, A., & Sommerstein, L. (1999). Literacy before and after inclusion in general education settings: A case study. *Journal of the Association for Persons with Intellectual Handicaps, 24*, 5–22.

Ryndak, D. L., Taub, D., Jorgensen, C., Gonsier-Gerdin, J., Arndt, K., Sauer, J., Ruppar, A., Morningstar, M. E., & Allcock, H. (2014). Policy and the impact on placement, involvement, and progress in general education: Critical issues that require rectification. *Research and Practice for Persons with Severe Disabilities (RPSD), 39*(1), 65–74. doi:10.1177/1540796914533942

Sacramento City Unified Sch. Dist. v. Holland, 14 F.3d 1398 (9th Cir.), cert. denied, 512 U.S. 1207. (1994).

Sailor, W., & McCart, A., (2014). Stars in alignment. *Research and Practice for Persons with Severe Disabilities, 31*(1), 55–64.

Sarason, S., & Doris, J. (1979). *Educational handicap, public policy, and social history.* Free Press.

Sauer, J. (2013). What's behind the curtain? A family's search for an inclusive Oz. *The Review of Disability Studies, An International Journal, 9*(2), 41–53.

Sauer, J., & Albanesi, H. (2013). Questioning privilege in the special education process. *Understanding and Dismantling Privilege, 3*(1), 1–21.

Siperstein, G. N., Parker, R. C., Bardon, J. N., & Widaman, K. F. (2007). A national study of youth attitudes toward the inclusion of students with intellectual disabilities. *Exceptional Children, 73*(4), 435–455.

Skilton-Sylvester, E., & Slesaransky-Poe, G. (2009). More than a least restrictive environment: Living up to the civil covenant in building inclusive schools. *Perspectives on Urban Education, 6*(1), 32–37.

Smith, A., & Kozleski, E. B. (2005). Witnessing Brown: Pursuit of an equity agenda in American education. *Remedial and Special Education, 26*, 270–280.

Soto, G., Muller, E., Hunt, P., & Goetz, L. (2001). Critical issues in the inclusion of students who use augmentative and alternative communication: An educational team perspective. *Augmentative and Alternative Communication, 17*, 62–72.

Strieker, T., Salisbury, C., & Roach, V. (2001). *Determining policy support for inclusive schools.* Consortium on Inclusive Schooling Practices.

Taylor, S. (1988). Caught in the continuum: A critical analysis of the principle of the least restrictive environment. *Journal of the Association for the Intellectually Handicapped, 13*(1), 41–53.

Taylor, M. J., West, R. P., & Smith, T. G. (2006). *Indicators of school quality: The link between school environment and student achievement.* Center for the School of the Future. http://www.csf.usu.edu/research/isq_achievement.pdf

Test, D. W., Mazzotti, V. L., Mustian, A. L., Fowler, C. H., Kortering, L. J., & Kohler, P. H. (2009). Evidence-based secondary transition predictors for improving post-school outcomes for students with disabilities. *Career Development for Exceptional Individuals, 32*, 160–181.

Trent, J. W. (1994). *Inventing the feeble mind: A history of mental retardation in the United States*. University of California Press.

Turnbull, A. (1982). Preschool mainstreaming: A policy and implementation analysis. *Educational Evaluation and Policy Analysis, 4*, 281–291. doi:10.3102/01623737004003281

University of Kansas. (2015). *SWIFT center*. University of Kansas. http://www.swiftschools.org/

U.S. Department of Education. (2006, February 15). *Federal register*. National Institute on Disability and Rehabilitation Research—Notice of Final Long-Range Plan for Fiscal Years 2005–2009, Vol. 71, No. 31. Office of Special Education and Rehabilitative Services, Department of Education.

U.S. Department of Education. (1989). *Eleventh annual report to congress on the implementation of the education of the handicapped act*. https://archive.org/stream/eleventhannualreoounit/eleventhannualreoounit_djvu.txt

U.S. Department of Education. (2014). *Thirty-fifth annual report to congress on the implementation of the individuals with disabilities education act, 2013*. http://www2.ed.gov/about/reports/annual/osep/2013/parts-b-c/index.html

U.S. Department of Justice. (2015, July). *United States' investigation of the Georgia Network for Educational and Therapeutic Support, D.J. No. 169-19-71*. Washington, DC.

Wagner, M., Newman, L., Cameto, R., Levine, P., & Garza, N. (2006). *An overview of findings from wave 2 of the National Longitudinal Transition Study-2 (NLTS2)*. (NCSER 2006-3004). SRI International. http://www.nlts2.org/reports/2006_08/nlts2_report_2006_08_complete.pdf

Walczak v. Florida Union Free School District, 97-7155. (1998).

Wansart, W. L. (1995). Teaching as a way of knowing: Observing and responding to students' abilities. *Remedial and Special Education, 16*(3), 166–177.

Wehmeyer, M., & Agran, M. (2006). Promoting access to the general curriculum for students with significant cognitive disabilities. In D. Browder & F. Spooner (Eds.), *Teaching language arts, math, and science to students with significant cognitive disabilities* (pp. 15–37). Paul H. Brookes.

White, J., & Weiner, J. S. (2004). Influence of least restrictive environment and community-based training on integrated employment outcomes for transitioning students with intellectual disabilities. *Journal of Vocational Rehabilitation, 21*(3), 149–156.

Wisconsin Education Association Council. (2014). *Special education inclusion*. http://www.weac.org/Issues_Advocacy/Resource_Pages_On_Issues_one/Special_Education/special_education_inclusion.aspx

Zuna, N., & Turnbull, R. (2004). "Imagine all the people, sharing ..." or a (not so) modest proposal made on the eve of IDEA reauthorization. *Research and Practice for Persons with Severe Disabilities, 29*(3), 210–213.

CHAPTER 4

Exploring the Legacy of Steven Taylor
Editor and "Gentle Anarchist"

Geert Van Hove and Elisabeth De Schauwer

1   Introduction

University professors worldwide have three tasks: teaching, scientific research, and delivering (academic) service to society. Only a few academics can find for themselves a fruitful balance among those three tasks. Steven J. Taylor combined being the Director of the Syracuse University's Disability Studies program with the Directorship of the Center on Human Policy and his editorship of the journal *Mental Retardation* (later titled *Intellectual and Developmental Disabilities*; aka *MR/IDD*).

Faithful to his basic ideas, he worked from 1993 to 2011 on what he called "a somewhat unique journal."[1] The "multi-perspectivity" of the journal is significant within a field that for years had been studying "people with intellectual disabilities" from a "technical-clinical" angle. Steven Taylor encouraged submissions from colleagues who studied intellectual disabilities as a social and cultural phenomenon.

As editor, Taylor introduced a new style of "applied journal": no longer was research translated for the practice field. Taylor decided to work with a bottom-up strategy that gave place to "relevant issues of today." He introduced a new section in the journal called "Perspectives"; within this part he was looking for "thoughtful commentary from thoughtful people." He also tried to open up the journal for authors and topics "that matter." We will use this specific little phrase while introducing some articles as specific tools Taylor used to build his position as a "gentle anarchist." (The articles we will introduce are chosen—on a very subjective basis—from within the period of Taylor's editorship.)

Following this introduction, we will briefly clarify our view on "gentle anarchism." Next, we will present a number of articles that in our opinion could only appear in *MR/IDD* under Steven Taylor's editorship. These articles will help us to understand the fundaments of "gentle anarchism." In our conclusion we will show that Steven Taylor's dedication to the principles of gentle anarchism helped to prepare the development of disability studies.

© KONINKLIJKE BRILL NV, LEIDEN, 2021 | DOI: 10.1163/9789004471856_005

1.1 "Gentle Anarchism": What's in a Name?

The first author to describe gentle anarchism (Verwulgen, 2015) framed it as "a conscious form of naivety and social positioning, an unrestrained ethics of play and a pledge for measures that hand over control to stimulate spontaneous interaction and engagement and to be liberated from various impasses" (p. 198).

First, gentle anarchists stand out because they very consciously take up a position away from a sort of "middle-of-the-road thinking" based on (too?) many compromises that paralyze openings for change. His confrontation with otherness demands a different becoming as it challenges the pre-existing order of what a human being *should* be. People like Taylor use a number of strategies that help to establish the afore-mentioned positioning; e.g., the use of a kind of "playfulness" to unmask a middle-class/bourgeois-type seriousness. Furthermore, self-criticism is used to expose one's own middle-class seriousness. Also, a great deal of "companionship" stands out with peers and other pioneers. As Davies (2006, pp. 436–437) argued: "Our responsibility lies inside social relations and inside a responsibility to and for oneself in relation to the other—not oneself as a known entity, but oneself in process, unfolding or folding up, being done or undone, in relation to the other, again and again."

Secondly, a "gentle anarchist" shows more interest in what happens in the margin rather than taking shelter in the safety of the center. He is interested in processes of in- and exclusion of people who are focused on surviving, who encounter a lot of barriers to participation, who are nobody's first choice to spend time with. He constantly problematizes the "obvious," the "real," the "taken for granted." He stays suspicious about how the world appears and the categories that we use to divide and manage it.

Finally, gentle anarchists find themselves in a permanent state of "vigilance"; often, they are the first to notice the movements announcing cracks in a bastion of power. Notions of ambiguity, uncertainty, and indeterminacy are at the core of his work and open up the potential for creative and refreshing ways of thinking and acting. His engagement is always searching for the possibility of transformation and exploration of multiple ways of making sense of what surrounds us. A single event can disturb an established order or set in motion a process; it happens uninvited. Experimentation concerns that which is not yet known; it concerns that which comes about, that which is new and that demands more than recognizing or representing truth.

Taylor embodies a consistent political project. Throughout his work he sees the possibilities of being relevant by investing in empowerment, emancipation, and social justice. He criticizes and deconstructs binary ways of thinking, of dividing abled from disabled, and normal from abnormal (Meekosha

& Shuttleworth, 2009). Boundaries are not fixed between communities; he feels part of a movement, a collective movement to challenge the dominant discourse through which people with (intellectual) disabilities are read as 'less than human.' His work with people with a disability and their families is closely linked to activism, through which people with disabilities challenge their exclusion (Thomas, 2004).

We do not want this to sound easy or simple. Undoing ableism is hard work. McRuer (2006) was convinced: "Fundamentally structured in ways that limit access for people with disabilities, institutions perpetuate able-bodied hegemony, figuratively and literally constructing a world that always and everywhere privileges very narrow (and ever-narrowing) conceptions of ability" (p. 151). Often we are short of language for this kind of work. Sometimes certain ways of rethinking disability remain unspeakable and unspoken. We perceive an actual absence of words in the vocabulary to describe certain kinds of disability, of difference. All the time Taylor is pushing to unsettle, to disturb, to escape, to resist what is fixed, and is actively engaging in transformation of oneself and one's world without being caught in repressive discourses and practices.

1.2 Studying and Challenging the Power of Normativity

Segregation is part of daily life for people with disabilities, and lived experiences of exclusion are taken for granted. Far too many people with a disability are confronted with lower or no qualifications, unemployment, health problems, loneliness, or isolation from community life. The grand narrative of lack, tragedy, and deviance leads to pathology and passivity (Goodley & Rapley, 2001). For Taylor, it is a disturbing but everyday problem that in working with people with a disability he encounters people in key decision-making positions who categorize and dismiss people with disabilities as less than human—or at the very least as existing outside humanity as they understand it (Goodley & Runswick Cole, 2014). People with a disability are, for them, an incomprehensible other (Goodley, 2011). Campbell (2009) argued that disabled people are pathologized through the "production, operation, and maintenance of ableist-normativity" (p. 1).

In the field of disability, we tolerate, assume, and talk the language of correction, adaptation, rehabilitation, treatment, and normalization. Butler (2004) explained why this is so deeply engrained in each one of us: "Our very sense of personhood is linked to the desire for recognition, and that desire places us outside ourselves, in a realm of social norms that we do not fully choose, but that provide the horizon and the resource for any sense of choice that we may have" (p. 33). The forces of normalization produce—through language, structure, discourse, and practice—the very terms through which we become recognizable, as human, as a particular kind of human, or as less than human, as a viable or a non-viable subject (Davies, 2012). We would like to present the "social construction of humanness" (Bogdan & Taylor, 1989, p. 135) as a pendula: as we construct, we are being constructed.

Taylor thinks and works "one foot in and one foot out" (Macedo in Freire, 1985, p. 178), just like Freire. We cannot keep out of academia, even when it is one of the institutions that is very exclusive and a status symbol for keeping the social order intact. We are agents of what we do, so Taylor invests in working collectively and politically in changing the world.

2   Unraveling the Articles in Mental Retardation

Let's have a look at the articles as tools for meaningful concepts that served our gentle anarchist well.

2.1   *Lines of Flight*

Regularly, Steven Taylor takes up a position in such a way that "lines of flight" become visible, allowing leaving the "mainstream." A line of flight is a concept developed by Deleuze and Guattari (Deleuze & Guattari, 1987). In the translation from the French "ligne de fuite," the translator notes that in French "fuite" covers more than the act of fleeing; it also means flowing, leaking, and disappearing in the distance. They made small ruptures in everyday habits of thought and initiated minor dissident flows (Roy, 2003, as cited in Gough, 2006, p. 63). Deleuze acknowledged and subverted certainties: "He affirms the possibilities of becoming something else, beyond the avenues, relations, values, and meanings that seem to be laid out for us by our biological make-up, our evolutionary heritages, our historical/political/familial allegiances, and the social and cultural structures of civilized living" (Sotirin, 2005, p. 99).

Steven Taylor made sure authors got the possibilities with their articles to break through the cracks in the systems that controlled some "chapters of the field." Through publications in the journal they were able to find allies for their innovative ideas. With their articles they reinvented some of the chapters in the field while showing creative new trajectories. So a line of flight is not "against" the mainstream: it orients away from the controlling ideas. A great example of such a line of flight can be found in the article of David Smukler (2005) in which he fought the assumption that autism is a result of a "theory of mind deficit." By uncovering the historical roots of the concept—the first use of the term "theory of mind" goes back to primatologists bringing the question

"Does the chimpanzee have a theory of mind?" on the table—he started to build a very critical text showing that the experts using this term for children with autism (Baron-Cohen, 2001; Leslie & Frith, 1988) were going back to the same "false belief task" colleagues developed for chimpanzees. In developing their work, Baron-Cohen and his colleagues described that the heart of autism can be found in the idea that children can't understand that others have perspectives. This mind blindness and the inability to mind read others makes children with autism as children lacking a theory of mind. Smukler (2005) discovered that:

> ... the "theory of mind" theory shares eight characteristics with earlier representations of autism:
> 1. Its proponents view autism as a unitary phenomenon that results from a single, core disability.
> 2. Its adherents claim to have the professional authority to explain autism.
> 3. They assert a scientific basis for such claims.
> 4. Autism is portrayed as exotic and extreme.
> 5. Autism is represented not as difference but as deficiency (those with autism are "damaged").
> 6. The intelligence of autistic people is often regarded as questionable or entirely discounted.
> 7. Professionals and other helpers are depicted as endlessly patient while autistic people are rarely viewed as patient.
> 8. All of the above is normalized, such that it becomes a dominant perspective that is not questioned ... (p. 14)

In a reaction to these eight characteristics, Smukler (2005) observed that the "theory of mind" seems to be "mind blind" itself while ignoring the autistic experience:

> Ultimately, the question of who has the privilege to define autism is not a scientific but a philosophical and political one .... Alternate constructions are possible when autistic voices are made part of the discourse .... A process of including first-person perspectives of autistic people is the only way that definitions based on difference rather than deficits will emerge to change negative social constructions of autism .... A commitment to democratic and inclusive communities requires a process of communicative partnership that elicits narratives based on all voices, even those that are difficult to decipher .... (p. 22)

Taylor consciously searches for/makes use of what happens in the margin (Dalea & Robertson, 2004). For Taylor, this is more interesting than studying the center. As De Sousa Santos made clear, the insights into our condition are more likely to come not from the center(s of power) but rather from the marginalized periphery; from those who on a daily basis experience domination, poverty, and social injustice. To this end, Steven Taylor used an article about a controversial topic, in which the author made use of a controversial research method (auto-ethnography). In a time when research on parents with intellectual disabilities was still in its infancy (see, e.g., Tymchuck, 1991, 1992; Feldman et al., 1986) he made possible the publication of "On Loving and Hating My Mentally Retarded Mother," by Carol Rambo (1997), professor of sociology at the University of Memphis. With this very controversial article Taylor opened up possibilities to explore the margin. Some statements were made which could at least be called very notable for the year 1997:

- The article stated that some persons with an intellectual disability have children, whereas in former days those people were seen as "eternal children."
- The article sketched situations that point to (sexual) abuse (pp. 422–423). Considering the auto-ethnographical nature of the text, the details of the facts and the dialogues hit hard.
- In the course of the article it became clear how the main character of the article struggled with extremely conflicting emotions (see, e.g., p. 428): "... I still need a mommy and I'll never have one. All I have is her ...." Parents who don't realize that fever is very dangerous, but have uncontrollable fits of laughter with their children; parents who on the one hand forbid you to play with good friends, but on the other hand with childish enthusiasm gather things on the street left behind after a carnival parade. Those well-chosen critical incidents in the article teach us that rights of children must never have less attention than the "right to parenthood."
- Indirectly, the identity of the author of this auto-ethnographic document proved that children of parents with intellectual disability can be very intelligent: Carol Rambo was encouraged by her uncle, aunt, social workers, and teachers and became a professor of sociology.
- By means of this article Taylor launched the message that "postmodern ethnographic reporting" is essential for a better understanding of the underlying multiple and complex layers of a phenomenon such as "parents with an intellectual disability."

In earlier days Taylor himself wrote an extraordinary chapter on this subject, entitled "Children's Division Will Come to Take Pictures" (1995). In this chapter he clearly chose the side of the Duke family. He described the family not from an "expert position" but from a relationship of many years which made him an "insider" who looks with a mild eye at what happened in the family. In order to appreciate the Duke family, one has to juxtapose how they look from the outside—that is, from a distance—with how they look from the inside—how they see themselves and how they look once one has gotten to know them well.

2.2 A Kind of Playfulness

Taylor very consciously introduced a "kind of playfulness" to question the establishment, wallowing in a sort of middle-class/bourgeois-type seriousness. "To imagine is to consider desire, to dream of possibilities, to see life differently" (Campbell, 2009, pp. 19–20). In line with Kane (2004), Taylor noticed that creativity has come to be seen as one of the most precious human assets. Playfulness seems to enhance creativity and exploration. Play is the sort of progressive, imaginative, ritualistic, frivolous, and cosmic activity that allows us to be energetic, imaginative, and confident in face of an unpredictable, contestive, and emergent world. Is it possible to imagine disability outside of the context of tragedy or catastrophe?

The most obvious example of the introduction of "playfulness" can be found in the article "Inquiry Cantos" by Phil Smith (2001). Prior to the publication of this article, Smith had long tried to criticize "the" way we represent disabled bodies, among others by controlling the language that we use, by questioning it and by introducing it in a playful manner and from the conviction that "… the flowers of rhetoric have real power to change reality, to penetrate it through and through, to 'split rocks'" (Franke, 2000, in Smith, 2006, p. 33).

In "Inquiry Cantos," Smith stated that:

> Responding to what has been called the postmodern turn some Disability Studies Scholars are choosing to represent their work in alternative textual formats including poetry and fiction. These texts , representing multiple subjectivities, offer ways to explicate, problematize, and reconstruct new ways of understanding so-called developmental disability that are complex and plural … (2001, p. 379)

In his "Second Canto: Song of Words," Smith (2001) explored this "playfulness." In doing so he referred to the word "scherzando," "a word used to describe to a performer the mood or tone of a musical passage. It tells the performer to be playful, literally to leap with joy …" (Smith, 2001, p. 380).

Prior to this, in 1999, when he wrote "Food Truck's Party Hat," Smith decided to follow Patti Lather, when she incited creation of a laboratory in which to explore textual possibilities for telling stories that belong to others. Even then,

Smith stated (1999), "I knew that I wanted to play with those textual possibilities as a way of discovering new metaphors and to acknowledge and invite the audience/reader into a more active, transactional role with text ..." (p. 245). At the same time Smith feels that collecting and telling stories can never be neutral, because writing/telling is always a political act. In doing so Smith linked "playfulness" to an appeal by McLaren (1995) to construct an anti-colonial, anti-racist, and liberatory dialectics of hearing, touching, and tasting the other beyond their inscription in colonial texts. To illustrate this, we refer to Smith's "Second Canto: Song of Words" (2001, pp. 380–381):

Second Canto: Song of Words

Moron
Imbecile
Idiot
Retard mildly
      moderately
      severly
      profoundly abnormal
            deviant
            pathological
            incompetent time-out
                  antecedent
                  modification
                  consequence nonverbal
                        low-functioning
                        vegetative
                        sheltered workshop

total care
group home
training school
supervised apartment toileting
            pre-vocational
            telephone use
            bed-making IPP
                  ICF/MR
                  SIB
                  ABC   noncompliant
                        conduct disorder
                        oppositional   inclusion

> seclusion
> intrusion
> illusion
> collusion
> exclusion
> delusion

In later publications Smith (2006, 2008) tried to create (in his own words)

> an undiscovered set of metaphors to unpack "ed DUCAT ion scanty science." A spoken/written langue/tongue piece based on an intentionally outlandish and overwhelming form used by (some) conceptual, and POST poets. Avoiding the never transparent language that inscribes the offalic and violent taxonomy of norm(&)al academic research Repres©entation, this writ(h)ing outlines, through a flagantry and literally/littoraly entirely tiresome, unspeakably visual and aural word conflagation, a po-etic that begins to de-inscribe the nature of metaphoric, medicalized, ventriloquizing, normative discourse of social science/education. (2008, p. 706)

In 2006, Smith gave himself and us four tasks which are essential to understand the link between playfulness and political responsibility.

– We need new tongues/new languages of dis-ability, new speakings about normal, new kinds of texts that can Re-present.
– We need a different kind of ideology: a shift from the ideology of normalcy, from the rule and hegemony of normates, to a vision of the body (and mind) as changeable, unperfectable, unruly and untidy.
– We will need a new kind of research … a kind that will be counter to typical academic exploration … Research that is irregular, research that is nonlinear, research that is artistic, research that is irrational.
– And it all will be done by those whose voices and signs and silences and lives have not been heard or seen or attended by the normative (educational) institutions in our culture …. (pp. 56–58)

2.3   *Importance of Connection, Connecting, Connected*

Our identity is in constant becoming—rhizomatic, nomadic, a constant journey with no final destination. We are never still, always relational, always to come, always to connect, it is about AND … AND … AND … "Connectivity is a potential to uncover new and varied ways of becoming and considering how things could be otherwise. Instead of resisting connectivity, the project could be to explore and appreciate differences: becoming other(s) in multiple ways, a multiplicity of flowing connections mad, released and reformed" (Gibson, 2006, p. 195). Every subject is caught up in multiple, connective assemblages that are in continuous change. Thinking in terms of connections and assemblages is a useful way to look at the participation of persons with a disability. It is not only depending on their capacities but also on their possibilities to make alliances. The social networks shape their becoming as human beings, and are situated in a rhizomatic proliferation of connections and temporary points of assemblage. These connections and organizations of connections are necessary to exist for all of us. Taylor acknowledges the importance of interconnectedness. He acknowledges that our lives and relations are interconnected for, with, and in communities. It always begins with what you bring, what you have learned, what you contribute. He understands in thinking and working together, as a scholar and as a human being, the importance of "we" and to speak collectively.

The best example can be found in the article "The Feeling of Power and the Power of Feelings," about the inaccessibility of academic texts within disability studies. Steven Taylor opened up a forum for Nancy Rosenau, making sure there was space for indirect self-critique. Rosenau (2004) described the contrast between a rights-based theorization of disability with a corresponding "feeling of power" with a relationship-based theorization of disability with its corresponding "power of feelings": "I am saying that the rest of us miss out on some moving ideas if they are not translated and made available for wider consumption and conversations where they can touch, disturb, and inspire ..." (p. 264).

Rosenau (2004) argued for a relationship-based agenda as a complement to a rights-based agenda. She is convinced that a rights-based agenda holds an unsharable them/us agenda (p. 266). The kind of relationship Rosenau discussed featured closeness, commitment, respect, support, and humor, in contrast with stereotypes such as risk, dependent, passive, helpless, sick, and in need of care. If we want to carry forward the meaningful practice of inclusion, we need relationships in addition to rights (p. 267). She continued:

> It was feelings that motivated life-changing decisions for institutionalized children, not awareness of abrogated rights and not feelings of compassion but feelings of connection, feelings of relational attachment. A rights agenda that invokes a power analysis rightly challenges hierarchical social arrangements. Power describes relationships as positions. A relational approach describes relationships as feelings and invokes a different analysis that focuses on subjective internal experience. The power analysis engages the head; the relational analysis engages the heart. I am not arguing either/or but both/and ... We, real-world practitioners,

could benefit from importing ivory tower theorizing and discover that big words and big ideas have a place in everyday life. (pp. 269–270)

As a gentle anarchist Taylor seemed to be very loyal in giving credit to companions and fellow pioneers. In this matter we refer to the pioneering spirit of Taylor himself and his Center on Human Policy. Even before one talked about disability studies at all, Taylor himself was at the base of the matter with actions like "label jars not people" and articles on the "social construction of humanness." Taylor formed, but was also formed by his great teacher Burton Blatt, who was a pioneer in humanizing services for people with disabilities. Blatt initiated community-living programs and family support services. He was the author of the publication *Christmas in Purgatory* (1966), which brought attention to the abuse of people with disabilities in institutions.

Starting from this sphere of influence, it soon became evident that Taylor kept defending his companions from the very first beginning (e.g., Robert Bogdan and Douglas Biklen), even when these companions came under attack by critics. For instance, Douglas Biklen was regularly criticized when he rejected the old ways of thinking about communication used by speech therapists and looked for "alternative communication methods" like facilitated communication. By publishing the article "A Validated Case Study of Facilitated Communication" (Salomon Weiss et al., 1996), Taylor showed not only his loyalty to his companion, but also made clear that reporting on solid and repeatable scientific research on the function of this method was extremely important. With this decision, Taylor's research remained in line with that of his teacher Blatt and asked the question: How can we support people who (literally) have no voice today in such a way that they are capable of sharing their view with us? This article proved that, if you want to do this, new methods (e.g., facilitated communication) will have to be applied and new paths will have to be thoroughly documented and investigated: It is the child in the research that will express his meaning, not the facilitators.

2.4   *Curiosity about What Is Not-Yet-Known*

With the article "Creation of an Autistic Identity Through Online Communication" (2006), Taylor proved to be very vigilant to new ways of thinking and 'alternative' practices in the field. This activity is driven by desire, doubt, interest, and leads to more questions instead of finding "right" answers.

Through an article by Bronlow and O'Dell (2006), readers of *Mental Retardation* received information about the power of internet chatrooms vis à vis the "autism community." With the new online possibilities, people with autism used the benefits of computer-mediated communication. As such a strong new link was built between the new technologies and the self-advocacy movement. While analyzing empirical material from such internet discussions, the authors illustrated two discussions:

- The first centered on the questions "Who are the experts?" and "Who has the knowledge about autism?" From the discussions it became clear that people with autism should be considered as the most important experts. This statement brings the discussion about the tension between scientific and first-hand experiential knowledge to the table (p. 318).
- The other part of the discussion showed the possibilities of membership of such an online discussion group for the identity-building of the participants. The online tool became a safe space to discover the differences of the members with neurotypicals: "... to accept ourselves as AS, we need to know how we differ from NTS ...." (p. 319).

This article can be linked to Judith Butler's ideas on "subjectivation" and the importance of "citational chains." It is precisely with this last concept that the impact of external powers (e.g., from experts) becomes clear when building up an identity. The territorializing lines of force through which binaries are established and maintained are not only or even primarily experienced as oppressive. We depend on them, and the lines of flight also depend on them. They "are comforting: they enable the chaos of the world to be reduced to discrete categories of meaning and structure. They are also necessary, for they enable us to interact with the social world; to form relations with others and to have a political 'voice'" (Malins, 2007, p. 153). *At the same time* they "reduce the range of connections a body can make with the world around it, diminishing its potential for difference and becoming-other" (Malins, 2007, p. 153). "It is through citational chains or repeated acts of recognition that we are subjected and subject ourselves to discourses that are prior to us and external to us" (Davies et al., 2013, p. 682). The citational chains enable the accomplishment of ourselves as recognizable human, autonomous beings with a viable sense of individual identity. "Subjection consists precisely in this fundamental dependency on a discourse we never chose but that, paradoxically, initiates and sustains our agency" (Butler, 1997, p. 2). Butler's subject is the site of reiteration, of repetition over time. "If conditions of power are to persist, they must be reiterated; the subject is precisely the site of such reiteration ..." (Butler, 1997, p. 16).

3   Conclusions

By positioning oneself in his role as editor, but also in his two other roles— teacher in/giving support to the community—as "gentle anarchist," Taylor helped to pave the way for disability studies, even before it existed as an interdisciplinary field. He presented the necessity of engaging with a plurality of perspectives if disability is to be conceived as a fully social and political phenomenon. In 2006, Taylor wrote a very illuminating article on the subject ("Before It Had a Name: Exploring the Historical Roots of Disability Studies in Education," p. XIII). In this text he listed a number of basic propositions to which he has always remained faithful—and this is considering the preceding analysis of his role as editor certainly a success.

- Disability is a creation, which makes the definition and representation of disability crucial. Disability is a social phenomenon that finds its meaning in social and cultural contexts (p. XIV).
- The above statement about disability leads to questioning "institutions" (based on an individual/pathological model) but also of the legitimacy of "special education" (p. XVII).
- Disability is not merely a label forced on people so defined; it can also be an identity or source of pride (p. XIX).
- To regard disability as a creation is not to deny variation. Variations according to ability do not need to be valued negatively or wrapped in stereotypes and stigma (pp. XIX–XX).

We never quite know how far this takes us, whom it reaches, how it changes, and when it is understood, but it presents us with multiple challenges and a continuing invitation for intense engagement, just like Steven Taylor demonstrated in his life. We like to remember him as a gentle anarchist and an intellectual giant with a larger, deeper, systemic, societal, and political project.

Note

1 For all direct quotes from Steven Taylor, see http://faculty.strose.edu/blacks/Intel&DevDisabilities.htm

References

Baron-Cohen, S. (2001). Theory of mind and autism. A review. *International Review of Research in Mental Retardation, 23*(23), 169–184.

Bogdan, R., & Taylor, S. J. (1989). Relationships with severely disabled people: The social construction of humanness. *Social Problems, 36*(2), 135–148.

Blatt, B., & Kaplan, F. (1966). *Christmas in purgatory: A photographic essay on mental retardation.* Human Policy Press.

Bronlow, C., & O'Dell, L. (2006). Constructing an autistic identity: AS voices online. *Mental Retardation, 44*(5), 315–321.

Butler, J. (1997). *The psychic life of power. Theories in subjection.* Stanford University Press.

Butler, J. (2004). *Undoing gender.* Routledge.

Campbell, F. K. (2009). *Contours of ableism.* Palgrave Macmillan.

Dalea, R., & Robertson, S. (2004). Interview with Boaventura de Sousa Santos. *Globalisation, Societies and Education, 2*(2), 147–160.

Davies, B. (2006). Subjectification: The relevance of Butler's analysis for education. *British Journal of Sociology of Education, 27*(4), 425–438.

Davies, B. (2012). *Normalization and emotion.* Paper presented at Mid-Sweden University, Sundsvall.

Davies, B., De Schauwer, E., Claes, L., De Munck, K., Van de Putte, I., & Verstichele, M. (2013). Recognition and difference: A collective biography. *International Journal of Qualitative Studies in Education, 26*(6), 680–691.

Deleuze, G., & Guattari, F. (1987). *A thousand plateaus. Capitalism and schizophrenia.* Continuum.

Feldman, M., Towns, F., Betel, J., Case, L., Rincover, A., & Rubino, C. (1986). Parent education project II: Increasing stimulating interactions of developmentally handicapped mothers. *Journal of Applied Behavior Analysis, 19*, 23–37.

Freire, P. (1985). *The politics of education.* Bergin & Garvey.

Gibson, B. (2006). Disability, connectivity and transgressing the autonomous body. *Journal of Medical Humanities, 27*, 187–196.

Goodley, D. (2011). *Disability studies: An interdisciplinary introduction.* Sage.

Goodley, D., & Rapley, M. (2001). How do you understand 'learning difficulties'? Towards a social theory of impairment. *Mental Retardation, 39*(3), 229–232.

Goodley, D., & Runswick-Cole, K. (2016). Becoming dishuman: Thinking about the human through dis/ability. *Discourse: Studies in the Cultural Politics of Education, 37*(1), 1–15. DOI: 10.1080/01596306.2014.930021

Gough, N. (2006). Shaking the tree, making a rhizome: Towards a nomadic geophilosophy of science education. *Education and Philosophy, 38*(5), 625–645.

Hickey-Moody, A., & Malins, P. (Eds.). (2007). *Deleuzian encounters: Studies in contemporary social issues.* Palgrave Macmillan.

Kane, P. (2004). *The play ethic: A manifesto for a different way of living.* Macmillan.

Leslie, A. M., & Frith, U. (1988). Autistic children's understanding of seeing, knowing and believing. *British Journal of Developmental Psychology, 6*(4), 315–324.

Malins, P. (2007). City folds, injecting drug use and urban space. In A. Hickey-Moody & P. Malins (Eds.), *Deleuzian encounters. Studies in contemporary social issues* (pp. 151–168). Palgrave MacMillan.

McLaren, P. L., & Giarelli, J. H. (1995). *Critical theory and educational research.* State University of New York Press.

McRuer, R. (2006). *Crip theory: Cultural signs of queerness and disability.* New York University Press.

Meekosha, H., & Shuttleworth, R. (2009). "What's so 'critical' about critical disability studies?" *Australian Journal of Human Rights, 15*(1), 47–75.

Rambo Ronai, C. (1997). On loving and hating my mentally retarded mother. *Mental Retardation, 35*(6), 417–432.

Rosenau, N. (2004). The feeling of power and the power of feelings: Theorizing in everyday life. *Mental Retardation, 42*(2), 263–271.

Salomon Weiss, M. J., Wagner, S. H., & Bauman, M. L. (1996). A validated case study of facilitated communication. *Mental Retardation, 34*(4), 220–230.

Sotirin, P. (2005). Becoming-woman. In C. Stivale (Ed.), *Gilles Deleuze. Key concepts.* Acumen.

Smith, P. (1999). Food truck's party hat. *Qualitative Inquiry, 5,* 244–261.

Smith, P. (2001). Inquiry cantos: Poetics of developmental disability. *Mental Retardation, 39*(5), 379–390.

Smith, P. (2006). Split—ting the ROCK of Speci(ES)al e.ducat.ion. FLOWers of lang(ue)age in>Dis<ability Studies. In S. Danforth & S. Gabel (Eds.), *Vital questions facing disability studies in education* (pp. 33–61). Peter Lang.

Smith, P. (2008). An ILL/ELL ip(op)tical po–ETIC/EMIC/Lemic/litic post* uv ed DUCAT ion recherché repres©entation. *Qualitative Inquiry, 14,* 706–722.

Smukler, D. (2005). Unauthorized minds: How "theory of mind" theory misrepresents autism. *Mental Retardation, 43*(1), 11–24.

Taylor, S. (1995). Children's division is coming to take pictures. In S. Taylor, R. Bogdan, & Z. M. Lutfyia (Eds.), *The variety of community experience.* Paul Brookes Publishing.

Taylor, S. (2006). Before it had a name: Exploring the historical roots of disability studies in education. In S. Danforth & S. Gabel (Eds.), *Vital questions facing disability studies in education* (pp. xiii–xxiii). Peter Lang.

Thomas, C. (2004). How is disability understood? An examination of sociological approaches. *Disability & Society, 19*(6), 569–583.

Tymchuck, A. (1991). Assessing home dangers and safety precautions: Instruments for use. *Mental Handicap, 19*(1), 4–10.

Tymchuck, A. (1992). Predicting adequacy of parenting by persons with mental retardation. *Child Abuse and Neglect, 16,* 165–178.

Verwulgen, H. (2015). *Alles is er, niets staat vast. Onderwijs en opvoeding, een bewegend standpunt.* Cyclus.

CHAPTER 5

To Keep, to Thrive, to Build in Community

Nancy Rice

> We will thrive if we keep alive what is distinctive about us as a community that combines scholarship and advocacy in the service of social justice for people marginalized by disability.
> STEVE TAYLOR

∴

1   Introduction

Steve Taylor's scholarship and advocacy spanned over 3 decades and examined both sides of several coins: human abuse and humanitarianism; institutions and community living; inclusion and exclusion; acceptance and rejection. In this chapter, I look at Steve's theoretical roots in Sociology and his broad application of them to the field of disability, all of which demonstrate his commitment to creating a more humane society.

2   Intellectual Heritage

Steve began his career as a researcher, in the early 1970's, about the time deinstitutionalization was moving into full swing; his context was the Center on Human Policy at Syracuse University, headed, at that time, by Burton Blatt. Nearly a decade earlier, Blatt and Kaplan (1966) had written *Christmas in Purgatory,* an exposé on a large institution in New York that housed people labeled mentally retarded.

In his dissertation, for which he spent many hours over 3 years as a participant-observer in institutions for people with labels of mental retardation, he acknowledged his mentor, Burton Blatt, "for his humanity." He acknowledged his colleague, Douglas Biklen, "for his political activism and perspectives;" and "especially," he recognized Robert Bogdan, his dissertation chair, "for teaching me his brand of sociology and for his intellectual integrity" (Taylor, 1977, preface). The two would go on to co-author many articles, one book, and co-edit 2 volumes of collected studies.

Steve and Bob were among the first to interview people with labels of intellectual disabilities (Bogdan & Taylor, 1982). They also interviewed people with and without disability labels, who were engaged in relationships with one another (Taylor & Bogdan, 1989). From these studies they created a framework they called "The Sociology of Acceptance" (Taylor & Bogdan, 1989). Taylor and others from the Center on Human Policy toured dozens of human service agencies around the United States. They described what community integration looked like in various contexts (Taylor, Biklen, & Knoll, 1987; Bogdan & Taylor, 1990; Taylor, Bogdan, & Racino, 1991).

2.1   *Theoretical Roots*

Steve's intellectual genealogy as a sociologist is key to understanding his worldview and the lens through which much of his scholarship is filtered. In classes and in his writings (e.g., Bogdan & Taylor, 1982, 1990; Taylor & Bogdan, 1989), Steve referenced the importance of Goffman's work. Goffman, a sociologist, wrote two books that became influential in the field of mental retardation: *Asylums* and *Stigma*.

Asylums was written after Goffman spent a year in an institution for those with mental illness. He coined the term "total institution," which was a defined as a place where inmates eat, sleep, work, and engage in other activities, isolated from others physically and socially (Goffman, 1961). Goffman found that individuals in such settings are stripped of their identity, and the management of the institution makes attending to the needs of residents difficult. This work was one of the first that looked at institutions from a perspective other than that of the medical field. It was also among the first that led to calls to close psychiatric institutions. Steve drew many parallels between this work and his own observations in institutions in his dissertation (Taylor, 1977).

In *Stigma*, Goffman focused on the ways in which people try to manage their public identity. In cases where a low value is ascribed to a characteristic or experience, for example, having spent time in prison or other type of institution, people will try to hide that fact, thus working to improve the way they are viewed by others. This concept was important in the lives of individuals who left institutions and negotiated their place in the community.

Another important sociological theory that underlies much of Steve's work is labeling theory. In sociology, labeling theory was originally developed in relation to the construct of 'deviance' (Becker, 1963). The idea is that there is no act that is intrinsically 'deviant,' but rather, 'deviance' is constructed as a process of the interactions between individuals and groups about norms, rules, and laws in any given society. Taylor and Bogdan (1976, 1982) used the same idea to reconceptualize 'mental retardation' as a social construct, in contrast to a fixed and unchangeable entity that resides within people so-labeled.

In 1966, Berger and Luckman published *The Social Construction of Reality*, which was one of the most influential sociological texts of the 20th century (International Sociological Association, 1998). This theoretical perspective argues that the meanings of all constructs—not just deviance—are the product of interpersonal and group interactions and agreements. The foundation of much of Taylor's work can be traced to these sociological theories and ideas that became prominent during the 1960's and 1970's.

2.2   *Methodological Branches*

Social Science methods of qualitative field research—observation in natural settings, in depth interviews—were not new in the second half of the 20th century; however, their application to the Human Service fields was. Goffman's *Asylums* is a classic example of this application.

Coupled with the social construction of reality, Taylor and Bogdan were able to unravel and better understand the meanings of 'mental retardation,' 'care,' 'institutions,' 'friendship,' and 'community life' from a variety of perspectives. Their research was among the first to look at first-hand accounts of what it means to live with a label of 'mental retardation' and not to 'interpret' those accounts from the perspective of a human service professional ("the Judges"), but rather, to let the person interviewed speak for him/herself. This was a brand new approach to research in the social sciences. What makes it even more compelling, even these many years later, is that the authors listened and took seriously the perspectives of those they termed "the Judged" (Bogdan & Taylor, 1976).

Participant-observation, in-depth interviews, case studies and stories of community experiences from a variety of perspectives were an important part of Taylor and Bogdan's research and advocacy. Their early work uncovered inhumane treatment of people and inconsistencies in human service policy; their later work was useful to researchers, practitioners, service providers, families, and people with disabilities to further the goal of community integration.

3   Groundbreaking Contributions

In this section, we will see how Steve and Bob Bogdan's theoretical foundations and research methods came together to create a substantive body of work to help us better understand people labelled 'mentally retarded' and how we can all live and work more closely in community.

3.1 Meet Pattie and Ed

In keeping with one of the most important goals of qualitative research, to understand the meaning of a construct, Steve and Bob Bogdan, were among the first to interview people with labels of mental retardation. Their book, *Inside Out*, is comprised mainly of transcripts of two individuals who the authors had met in their work in institutions. Ed Murphy and Pattie Burt had lived in a large state institution, but at the time of the interviews, each had moved into the community. Ed lived in a boarding house with 10 other men. Pattie had her own apartment at times, and at other times, lived with her mother or sister, or with a family that supported her. The transcripts are organized chronologically and largely speak for themselves. In the introduction, the authors ask the readers to keep an open mind in listening to the stories of Ed and Pattie. They remind us that the label of 'mental retardation' can be a barrier to truly hearing what they have to say. In keeping with qualitative methods, they note that in-depth interviews are the only way to really begin to understand the impact that labels have had on people to whom the labels have been attached.

Ed and Pattie's stories are compelling. They describe their childhood, the challenges of life in an institution, the pain of being left by their parents, the ups-and-downs of living with foster families, the struggles of working and living in the community, of getting along with others, what they look forward to and what brings them joy. Most days after work, Ed looked forward to going for a swim at the Y(MCA) to relax. Pattie looked forward to raising a family. Both Pattie and Ed described challenges they have faced in life: Ed described difficulties with focusing; Pattie gave several examples of her 'quick temper.'

What is unmistakable in these accounts are the feelings about common experiences that are easy to relate to, when unburdened by the label that typically separates labeled from non-labeled people. The ability to empathize with Pattie and Burt highlights our common humanity, and underscores our responsibility to respond to their humanness, not their label. At a societal level, it requires us to focus on the types of supports Ed and Pattie and others might need in order to thrive in the community.

3.2 The Sociology of Acceptance/The Social Construction of Humanness

Having challenged the construct of mental retardation in their interviews with Ed and Pattie, Taylor and Bogdan worked to reconstruct the meaning and implications of the term at both micro- and macro-levels. As I noted earlier, Taylor and Bogdan were writing in the context of the sociological theory of the day—specifically, theories that suggested that people with labels of mental retardation were 'deviant' and carried a 'stigma.' The specific meaning attributed to stigma included having 'questionable moral character' (Becker,

1963). These ideas were ubiquitous. Taylor & Bogdan wrote, "While the labeling approach to deviance has contributed significantly to our understanding of people with disabilities in our society, it has too often been interpreted in terms of the inevitability of rejection of people with obvious differences" (Taylor & Bogdan, 1989, p. 25).

Drawing on research conducted over 2 years, across 10 states, in a variety of agencies and homes for people with labels of mental retardation, with family members, and human service providers, Taylor & Bogdan (1989) explained that they had witnessed many instances of acceptance, rather than rejection, of people with disability labels; in particular, they focused on individuals with more significant disabilities. Accepting relationships were defined as: "relationships with a person with a deviant attribute, in this case mental retardation, and a non-disabled person, which is long-standing and characterized by closeness and affection and in which the deviant attribute, or disability, does not have a stigmatizing, or morally discrediting character in the eyes of the nondisabled person" (p. 27). Given the lack of descriptive studies that showed authentic relationships with 'deviant' individuals, Taylor and Bogdan used their platform to report on examples that countered the prevailing view that 'deviance' always results in exclusion. They noted the importance of describing and understanding these relationships in the service of creating a more inclusive society.

In terms of reconstructing or expanding ideas at the macro-level, the authors argued for research and understanding that was the other side of "A Sociology of Deviance." They noted that 'A Sociology of Acceptance'—their descriptive relationships were a beginning—was both practical and theoretical. The practical significance would be useful to human service workers and individuals in society who interact with people with disabilities. The theoretical work would lead to an understanding of how society can evolve to include those labeled 'different' or 'deviant.'

Bogdan and Taylor (1989) continued to investigate relationships between nondisabled individuals and people with significant disabilities—people who "drool, soil themselves, do not walk or talk" (p. 135). They were interested in understanding how these individuals constructed their friend or family member as "like us," when doctors and other professionals used terms like 'vegetable' to describe the same person, or did not attribute conscious thought to the person in question.

In close proximity and relationship with individuals with significant disabilities, the nondisabled partners observed changes in tongue movements or eye gaze, for example, and were thus able to attribute thought and expressions of preferences to individuals who had been dismissed by the medical community as being incapable of cognition or communication.

Nondisabled partners also attributed personality traits to their disabled friend or family member. They were described as being funny, silly, "a live-wire" or a "handful." Although changes in movements and vocalizations may be small, those in close relationship with individuals with significant disabilities were able to not only notice the differences, but also ascribed meaning to the changes, and attributed personality characteristics to the individual based on these. People with significant disabilities were also seen as providing nondisabled partners or family members with something important: companionship, an opportunity to provide care, or an opportunity to meet new people and learn about aspects of their community they would otherwise have not known about. Some spoke of more philosophical benefits they received from being in a relationship with a person with a significant disability: becoming more accepting of others, for example. In these ways, the relationship was viewed as reciprocal, in that both parties were giving something to the other.

Reporting on the relationships between nondisabled people and people with significant disabilities underscores the value of human beings who human service and medical professionals have labeled and thus lumped into a category; they do not know the person as an individual and have not taken the time to get to know them. Steve Taylor and Bob Bogdan pushed the boundaries to include deeper understanding of and advocacy for individuals with significant disabilities. Their work consistently reached out to the margins of society and pulled those most vulnerable into the center of their work.

3.3 *Life in the Community*

It seems a natural progression for Steve to have been the lead Series Editor on three volumes that focused on the experiences of people with disabilities living in the community. The Center on Human Policy, comprised of a committed staff and headed by Steve, won many grants to study community integration. The numerous studies and examples contained in these edited books were based on their extensive tours of community agencies, group homes, and participant observation in the lives of individuals and families who had children with significant disabilities. Their investigations took them across the country, to see programs in action and to talk at length with administrators, service providers, consumers, and their families. These volumes were written to aid practitioners in the work of integrating people with disabilities into community life.

Although clear(er) now, the understanding of 'community' as a social, rather than simply a geographic, space had to be clarified during the 1980's and 1990's. These volumes investigate what living in the community looks like from both macro (policy, funding) and micro (day-to-day, family life) perspectives. The studies consistently reflect the following principles that are the foundation of Community Integration (Taylor, 1987a): (1) All people with developmental disabilities belong in the community; (2) All people with developmental disabilities should be integrated into typical neighborhoods, environments, community settings; (3) Support should be given in families and typical homes; (4) We should encourage the development of relationships between people with developmental disabilities and other people; (5) We should give people with developmental disabilities opportunities to learn; and (6) Consumers and their families should be involved in the design, operation, and monitoring of services.

The first volume, *Community Integration for People with Severe Disabilities,* is divided into three parts: (1) Policy, principles, practice; (2) Leadership; and (3) With the People. Steve's contributions were in part 1: (1) a chapter on the Continuum Traps (discussed in another chapter in this volume) and (2) a chapter, with others, describing the ways that states were creating policies and funding mechanisms to have all children live in homes, and all adults live in the community. The chapter drew from site visits to 9 organizations across 5 different states. Consistent with Steve's focus, this chapter is subtitled "Community Integration for People with the Most Severe Disabilities" (Taylor, Racino, Knoll, & Lutfiyya, 1987).

The second volume focused specifically on organizations and the ways they support individuals in the community. Steve's individual contributions included three different studies: (1) a description of the State of Michigan's policies relative to permanency planning for children with disabilities and community integration for adults with disabilities, via a state-sponsored community service system (Taylor, 1991a); (2) a description and analysis of 3 counties in Wisconsin that were selected for their inclusion into the volume due to 3 criteria: (a) a willingness to serve people with challenging needs: (b) a commitment to community integration; and (c) active administrative leadership within each county, leading to possibilities for innovation (Taylor, 1991b); and (3) an analysis of person-centered planning that focused on individualized community living in some Wisconsin counties (Taylor, 1991c). Agencies in this study were supporting individuals in moving out of 6–8 person group homes.

The third volume focused on different ways in which agencies and individuals were creating inclusive spaces within communities: a bakery, a community choir, a public speaking course. These example were designed to be useful to practitioners, individuals and families to provide exemplars and stimulate reflection on ways to act that would have a similar impact in our own local community.

Steve's contribution to this volume was an insider's view into the life of the Dukes, a family in which both parents and both children had labels of mental retardation and other disabilities (Taylor, 1995). Steve was initially introduced to this family through a family support worker. He began as a participant observer, but developed a relationship with the family over time, helping them untangle bureaucratic webs related to Social Security benefits, with insurance companies, with schools and IEPs and with eviction notices. Steve was invited to the Dukes' family gatherings and was introduced by them as "a friend of the family." He spent many hours in and outside of their home, running errands, visiting friends, attending wrestling matches, or going grocery shopping.

Steve saw the ways in social service agencies interacted with the family. Specifically, during the years Steve spent with them, the family had been investigated by Child Protective Services four times. On one occasion, the father, Bill, had hit the daughter, Cindy, when she was a toddler. Steve reported that within the family and social networks, families sometimes reported on each other anonymously when they were feuding. Other instances of CPS involvement had to do with child neglect and a lack of housekeeping. While Steve noted that the family's child-rearing and housekeeping standards may not have been in keeping with middle-class values, the children were not in danger of abuse or neglect. The parents were adept at using their social networks to always have food and shelter, even when eviction loomed. They loved their children, valued their getting an education, spoke with them about careers and provided them with a family and social network upon which they could rely. In addition, their views of their children, and thus the identity they helped them create, was one of a typical person, not someone with a label of mental retardation. "In a society in which having a disability, and especially an intellectual disability is a stigmatizing and potentially discrediting characteristic (Bogdan & Taylor, 1994; Edgerton, 1967), this is no trivial parental contribution" (Taylor, 1995, p. 41).

Steve's reframing of the way the Dukes were viewed by service personnel was, and continues to be, an important contribution to the literature on understanding "disability" and the meaning of "service provision." He noted that navigating the tangle of paperwork involved in accessing Social Security benefits was never offered by service providers, in spite of the fact that such support was an essential aspect of their livelihood, and would have led to fewer transitions for the family.

3.4 Optimistic Research

Based on many of the studies in these 3 volumes, Bogdan and Taylor published an article in *Qualitative Sociology* entitled "Looking at the Bright Side: A Positive Approach to Qualitative Policy and Evaluation Research" (1990). In this article, they explained how they have woven several threads together: (1) staying true to a value position, that of community integration/inclusion for all, including those with the most significant disabilities; (2) application of rigorous research methods; and (3) creating a corpus of work that contains information and assistance for those who are working in the field of human services, specifically those working in the field of community integration.

Bogdan and Taylor described how they approach research, asking questions that are more 'optimistic.' For example, rather than asking whether moving people out of institutions 'works,' they focus on understanding the meaning of 'community inclusion,' or asking how it can be accomplished. The answers to these questions, they argue, are more useful to 'conscientious practitioners.'

This work was both a model and a catalyst for many researchers who focused on school inclusion during the 1980's and 1990's. During this time, numerous studies were published that reported on strong models of successful school inclusion and community integration. These studies didn't ask whether inclusion works, but *how* it works and how practitioners understand inclusion and related constructs.

3.5 *Ethical Considerations*

In an appendix to his dissertation (Taylor, 1977), and in an article 10 years later (Taylor, 1987b), Steve reflected on the ethics of participant observation in situations where harm is being done. What is the responsibility of the researcher in those situations? In Steve's case, should he have reported the attendants? Would it have done any good? Should he have left the field, and lost the opportunity to better understand how attendants in public institutions think about their work and the residents? His clear and thoughtful article discusses 4 possible options: (1) intervene; (2) leave the field; (3) blow the whistle; or (4) continue the study. He analyzed each option, noting there is not one right answer. In the end, the researcher has the responsibility to balance personal morality with professional ethics in making a decision.

When human abuse and suffering are involved, Steve argued, a researcher has an obligation to do *something*. In his humble way, Steve explains his actions: bringing reporters into backwards of institutions; testifying to legislative committees about human service options in the community; touring successful community agencies and reporting widely on these; meeting with consumers and parent groups to explain community options; and writing about community integration in both academic and mainstream outlets.

4 Conclusion

Steve Taylor's career coincided with significant changes in the understanding of and services for people with labels of mental retardation. Indeed, his work went a long way toward creating those changes. He used his academic position to impact the work and lives of many individuals: service providers, academics in the fields of mental retardation, special education, and general education, and especially, families and people with labels of mental retardation. In discussing the role of researchers, Steve wrote, "Participant observers have only tried to interpret the world; the point is to change it" (1977, p. 327). In so many ways, Steve Taylor's work and advocacy changed the world by making it a more humane place, especially those for whom he advocated so strongly.

Steve would be the first to say that there is still more work to do. In their article, noting that the knowledge base for inclusion is basically the same as that of special education, Danforth and Naraian (2015) suggest that the field of Inclusive Education create its own knowledge base. They tentatively suggest four foundational concepts for "This New Field of Inclusive Education:" (1) democracy; (2) interpersonal relationships communicating value; (3) political consciousness; and (4) situated agency. For each concept, they provided intellectual resources on which they are based. Bogdan and Taylor's article focused on relationships with people with significant disabilities, what they referred to as *the social construction of humanness* (1989) is the theoretical foundation *for interpersonal relationships communicating value*. In terms of thriving in the community, meaningful relationships are certainly a core value. Steve Taylor and Bob Bogdan were able to capture this essential piece of life through their research. That it is being used as a foundational concept to lay the groundwork for a body of knowledge to meaningfully create inclusive communities is a testament to Steve's lasting legacy.

References

Becker, H. (1963). *The outsiders: Studies in the sociology of deviance.* Free Press.

Berger, P. L., & Luckman, T. (1967). *The social construction of reality.* Doubleday.

Blatt, B., & Kaplan, F. (1966). *Christmas in purgatory.* Allyn & Bacon.

Bogdan, R., & Taylor, S. J. (1976). The judged, not the judges: Insiders' views of mental retardation. *American Psychologist, 31,* 47–52.

Bogdan, R., & Taylor, S. J. (1982). *Inside out: The social meaning of mental retardation.* University of Toronto Press.

Bogdan, R., & Taylor, S. J. (1989). Relationships with severely disabled people: The social construction of humanness. *Social Problems, 36*(2), 135–148.

Bogdan, R., & Taylor, S. J. (1990). Looking at the bright side: A positive approach to qualitative policy and evaluation research. *Qualitative Sociology, 13*(2), 183–192.

Danforth, S., & Naraian, S. (2015). This new field of inclusive education: Beginning a dialogue on conceptual foundations. *Intellectual and Developmental Disabilities, 50*(1), 70–85.

Goffman, E. (1961). *Asylums: Essays on the social situation of mental patients and other inmates.* Doubleday, Anchor Books.

Goffman, E. (1963). *Stigma.* Prentice-Hall.

International Sociological Association. (n.d.). *Top ten books of the century.* Retrieved February 29, 2016, from http://www.isa-sociology.org/books/books10.htm

Taylor, S. J. (1977). *The custodians: Attendants and their work at state institutions for the mentally retarded.* ProQuest Dissertations Publishing.

Taylor, S. J. (1987a). Introduction. In S. J. Taylor, D. Biklen, & J. Knoll (Eds.), *Community integration for people with severe disabilities* (pp. xv–xx). Teachers College Press.

Taylor, S. J. (1987b). Observing abuse: Professional ethics and personal morality in field research. *Qualitative Sociology, 10*(3), 288–302.

Taylor, S. J. (1991a). Toward families for all children. In S. J. Taylor, R. Bogdan, & J. A. Racino (Eds.), *Life in the community: Case studies of organizations supporting people with disabilities* (Vol. 1, pp. 19–34). Paul H. Brookes.

Taylor, S. J. (1991b). Community living in three Wisconsin counties. In S. J. Taylor, R. Bogdan, & J. A. Racino (Eds.), *Life in the community: Case studies of organizations supporting people with disabilities.* (Vol. 1, pp. 55–70). Paul H. Brookes.

Taylor, S. J. (1991c). Toward individualized community living. In S. J. Taylor, R. Bogdan, & J. A. Racino (Eds.), *Life in the community: Case studies of organization supporting people with disabilities.* (Vol. 1, pp. 105–112). Paul H. Brookes.

Taylor, S. J. (1995). "Children's division is coming to take pictures": Family life and parenting in a family with disabilities. In S. J. Taylor, R. Bogdan, & Z. M. Lutfiyya (Eds.), *The variety of community experience: Qualitative studies of family and community life* (pp. 9–22). Paul H. Brookes.

Taylor, S. J. (2009). *Acts of conscience: World War II, mental institutions, and religious objectors.* Syracuse University Press.

Taylor, S. J., Biklen, D., & Knoll, J. (Eds.). (1987). *Community integration for people with severe disabilities.* Teachers College Press.

Taylor, S. J., & Bogdan, R. (1989). On accepting relationships between people with mental retardation and nondisabled people: Towards an understanding of acceptance. *Disability, Handicap and Society, 4*(1), 21–36.

Taylor, S. J., Bogdan, R., & Lutfiyya, Z. M. (Eds.). (1995). *The variety of community experience: Qualitative studies of family and community life.* Paul H. Brookes.

Taylor, S. J., Bogdan, R., & Racino, J. A. (Eds.). (1991). *Life in the community: Case studies of organizations supporting people with disabilities* (Vol. 1). Paul H. Brookes.

Taylor, S. J., Racino, J., Knoll, J., & Lutfiyya, Z. (1987). Down home: Community integration for people with the most severe disabilities. In S. J. Taylor, D. Biklen, & J. Knoll (Eds.), *Community integration for people with severe disabilities* (pp. 36–66). Teachers College Press.

CHAPTER 6

A Bridge Too Far?

Teachers and Community Practice

Jennifer Randhare Ashton

1   Introduction

> As you looked across the gym, you could see both college students and community participants smiling as we danced, crafted, and played games. Why can't a classroom look this way too? Not only did the students we worked with have a great time, we did too! I feel that this sense of community I saw in our activity can be created in an academic setting. We created relationships. I believe that students of all backgrounds can build relationships with each other in the classroom. These relationships are impossible to grow if we segregate our special education and general education students. Schools need to realize how beneficial communities and inclusive classrooms can be. (Jillian, Teacher Candidate)

This statement from Jillian, a teacher candidate and student in my Introduction to Special Education class, is what I had always dreamed of hearing from students. Through the creation of a service-learning project for my teacher candidates and members of the community with developmental disabilities, I thought I had finally achieved something that had eluded me for years—getting teacher candidates to question the rationality of educational segregation. I believed that this was a first step toward understanding the complexity of inclusion, while recognizing the initial steps toward enacting this ideal were not always bound by complexity.

It was this particular experience that I planned to drawn upon when I agreed to write this chapter. Already familiar with some of Steven J. Taylor's work, I was honored to have my contribution included in a compilation of present day exemplars to attest to the enduring impact that he made. I assumed that since I shared his view that full community integration was integral to any discussion of educational inclusion the connections between his lifework and my service-learning project would be evident.

I excitedly amassed my collection of his work and started reading. As I read I began to think more critically about how Taylor's vision might be reflected in my service-learning project. The impact of immersing myself in his early work was surprisingly immediate, and almost jarring, as I attempted to articulate my thoughts while simultaneously plodding through the weekly tinkering of my service-learning project. I found myself reflecting not only on the current state of the project, but also on its development over the past few years.

This chapter traces the struggle that followed as I looked more closely at Taylor's work and was left doubting that sense of satisfaction I initially felt about my service-learning project. I will then explain how that pride quickly yielded to growing dissonance and self-doubt about a valued component of my teaching. I then wend my way back to a place of cautious optimism, fueled by discontent with an intractable structure and the need to persevere in my own spheres of influence. This is not intended to be an apology, but rather an acknowledgment of the value of returning to those powerful seminal intellectual influences that lead many contemporary scholars to persist in a slow march to reclaim the virtue and value of inclusion no matter how distant that goal remains.

Trained as a sociologist, Taylor was well aware that paradigmatic change needed time and that quick fixes would be difficult, if not impossible. Writing in 1987, Taylor, Racino, Knoll, Lutfiyya directly addressed the challenges of realizing this ideal in a world where segregation is seen as a viable, if not desirable option. They reminded that change takes place slowly, if at all, and with the assumed rationality of segregation it is not possible to simply decide to accommodate all people with developmental disabilities in integrated community-based settings. They further cautioned against leaving people in isolated segregated settings until such time as the perfect system of integration is formulated. These assertions left open the understanding that being committed to providing more integrated arrangements for people might mean accepting somewhat less integrated, or stopgap, settings on a temporary or transitional basis without apology as viable options to completely segregated programs. Trained as an educator, I wasn't acutely aware of this longitudinally-gauged sociological perspective and I found it to be simultaneously jarring and reassuring as I began this project.

2   Situating Segregation

The issue of segregation in education is complex and carries a long legacy. The history of the treatment of people with developmental disabilities, well documented by Taylor (2009), is marked with extreme marginalization and inhumane treatment that has created a narrative where people with the most significant disabilities are shunned from society and generally absent from regular community activities. In 1975, the Education of All Handicapped Children Act (PL 94-142) became law and the concept of Least Restrictive Environment (LRE) was constructed to rationalize a continuum of educational placements for people with developmental disabilities. This continuum makes it not only possible, but also logical to place students with the most significant support needs far away from their non-disabled peers in extremely segregated settings. Thirteen years later, Taylor (1988) systematically dismantled the assumed legitimacy of the LRE construct and advocated for an unconditional commitment to the integration of people with disabilities into all aspects of educational and residential life. In a 2004 review of Taylor's (1988) criticism of the continuum model, Nisbet (2004) noted that the continuum was so deeply embedded in education and human services that any changes at that time were minimal and largely in the subtler use of language rather than the actual placement of students.

As Taylor predicted, progress away from this model that legitimates segregation has been slow and the system has been incredibly resistant to change for over 30 years. Many people with developmental disabilities experience a segregated existence in the American public education system for their first 22 years and then negotiate the transition to equally segregated post-secondary systems of residential and occupational support for the remainder of their adult lives. Despite Taylor's logical and coherent plea, we are still debating LRE and where to 'put' students with disabilities instead of collaborating in IEP meetings to figure out how to provide necessary supports and services in integrated settings. The lack of progress that we've made in reaching Taylor's idealized goal is astounding.

3 Situating Myself

Through each phase of my career I struggled with the implicit segregation that existed between general and special education—for teachers and students alike. As a young educator and before I had the discursive language to articulate my discontent, I found the arbitrary boundaries that caused the segregation of so many students in special education to be mysterious and illogical. I had not yet thought critically about the role that the historical structure of the American education system played in this, let alone any possibility of my challenging it, but I had many questions. Ultimately, these questions fueled my professional journey from K-12 educator, through doctoral study, and into my current role as a teacher educator. I have spent the better part of my most recent academic career studying the faulty logic of special education and sharing that knowledge in my classes in an attempt to provide my teacher candidates with the critical understanding and language that eluded me early in my career. Through exposing the limitations and logical inconsistencies of the segregation of students with disabilities I seek to awaken in my teacher candidates an understanding of inclusion as a logical, necessary, and expected experience for all people with disabilities.

A short time into my doctoral study, I found Disability Studies in Education (DSE) to be a very useful lens through which I could begin to examine my long-held questions about special education. Disability Studies understands disability, not as a deficient trait found within an individual, but as a social, cultural, and political construct that finds meaning within a particular socio-cultural context (Taylor, 2011). A critical alternative perspective, DSE problematizes the traditional alliance of special education with positivist deficit medical models of disability that prioritize diagnosis and remediation over democratic education and social justice (Ashby, 2012; Rice, 2006; Slee, 2001; Ware, 2001, 2004). DSE challenges the traditional model (or discourse) of special education whereby an individual with a disability is identified as abnormal and in need of specialized treatment implemented by a specially trained individual, often in a segregated environment.

Selecting appropriate curriculum has been one of the biggest challenges I've faced in my teaching. It is a challenge made more complex given that my own pre-service program does not broadly embrace a DSE perspective and I must find ways to insert the DSE content into my courses myself.[1] Thankfully, my department is very welcoming of this perspective in my courses and I have not received any push-back from administration about my curricular choices.[2] Typical special education textbooks tend to reinforce deficit-based perceptions of disability and focus on all of the ways in which a student with disabilities is intrinsically flawed and in need of correction or cure. DSE scholars have long challenged the use of traditional textbooks that promote dehistoricized and decontextualized views of disability in seemingly rational and neutral ways while assuring adequate preparation for all teacher certification exams (Brantlinger, 2006; Slee, 1998). In my first semester at the college, I used one of these big glossy texts—a long-used resource for my course. It was a typical disability-of-the-week format Introduction to Special Education text from a major publisher and I supplemented it with a few other selected DSE readings of my choice. As the weeks went by I found myself criticizing the formulaic structure of the text and pointing out the ideological shortcomings of focusing on one disability at a time. By mid-semester my students were recognizing and criticizing the limitations of the structure and focus of the text and by the end of the semester the repetitive format had grown tiresome for all of us. Despite my efforts to provide a balance I found that I was using the text formulaically week to cover the disability classifications and struggling to carve out enough time to discuss the DSE scholarship to a satisfactory depth. I haven't used one of those big glossy textbooks since.

However, in today's assessment-obsessed educational climate the pressure to pass multiple costly state and national certification exams is high and the stakes are even higher. If the candidates do not pass these exams not only will they not be able to become teachers, but our preservice program will lose national recognition and cease to exist. The Council for Exceptional Children (CEC) sets national expectations for the preparation of special education teachers in the form of professional standards that drive pre-service curriculum, certification requirements, and certification exams—while adhering to a problematic deficit and medical model of disability (Ashton, 2011). By teaching to the CEC professional standards, I recognize that I am complicit in inculcating those same teacher candidates into the existing, but flawed, special education system. As such, I seek to find a delicate balance that ensures that the teacher candidates have the critical understanding necessary to question the assumed rationality of special education as well as a solid understanding of the structure within which they will someday work.

4   Situating My Course

Each semester I have the privilege of teaching two sections of Introduction to Special Education to teacher candidates who have just begun their professional journeys. The course is informed by professional experiences that include my own pre-service preparation, my earliest work as a general educator and later, as a special educator, up to my most recent experiences as a teacher educator.

I have structured the first half of my course to set a foundation for critical understanding of disability using the work of other DSE scholars to address topics that include the history of exclusion in special education (Valle & Connor, 2010), presuming competence (Biklen & Burke, 2006), humanistic and positive approaches to understanding behavior (Danforth, 2014; Smith, 2014; Orsati, 2016), institutional ableism (Lalvani & Broderick, 2013), the social construction of difference (Sapon-Shevin, 2014; Slesaransky-Poe & Garcia, 2014), and practices to advance critical hope embedded in classroom practice (Ware, 2001, 2004). I use a mix of research, commentary, and first-person narratives to introduce concepts that might be new to the teacher candidates in order to disrupt their personal understandings of disability.

In the second half of the course I teach about the processes and procedures of special education, while maintaining a focus on the DSE scholarship that grounded our earlier work. In preparation for state certification exams, we study the policies, processes, and procedures of special education, while still keeping the DSE concepts from the first half of the semester in the forefront of our consciousness. We study the social and educational consequences of LRE, while I strive to create a type of cognitive dissonance that helps the teacher candidates to question the rationality that special education perpetuates. I speak candidly with my teacher candidates about my own journey of understanding inclusion and the challenges that we face as current and future educators. Course feedback over the years has led me to believe that the teacher candidates appreciate my honesty and the critical perspectives presented in my class.

However, changing the way that my teacher candidates thought about disability was no small task. In relation to special education, teachers tend to make biased assumptions about an individual with a particular disability label based on what they think they know about that label, rather than what they actually know about the student as an individual (Ashby, 2012). With no required fieldwork in my class, I initially struggled with the limitations that this placed on my ability to challenge their preconceived notions of disability and their future work as educators. Not surprisingly, I found that their understandings about disability were deeply engrained aspects of their worldviews and reified by their personal experiences with disability.

Despite my introduction of DSE scholarship into the course, I found that it was difficult to shift my teacher candidates' beliefs in any meaningful way. I knew that I had to integrate experiences that would help them recalibrate their personal understanding of disability, normalcy, and belonging. Service learning seemed like the perfect way to bring these necessary experiences. When integrated into pre-service education programs, service learning has been found to influence teacher candidates' pedagogy, professional dispositions, commitment to teaching, and caring and sensitivity to student differences (Stringfellow & Edmunds-Behrend, 2013), which is precisely what I wanted. Five years ago, I added a service-learning project to my Introduction to Special Education course in a collaboration with individuals with developmental disabilities from the local community who came to the college to interact and socialize with my teacher candidates.

5 Community Partners

The organization I recruited as collaborators was Together Including Every Student (TIES). TIES is a community-based support program that promotes the participation of students and young adults who have developmental disabilities in inclusive, organized extracurricular and community activities through the support of trained peer volunteers. Traditionally affiliated with public school districts, TIES participants join activities where they can develop their recreational interests, learn about their community, and have fun with peers with and without disabilities. The TIES Program Director was excited to facilitate this collaboration between TIES and the College. I envisioned that the TIES service learning project had the potential to benefit both the teacher candidates and community participants as both populations are given opportunities to interact with and learn from each other in an integrated and informal setting. With most of the disabled community participants being aged 16 and older and the teacher candidates aged 18 and older, the opportunity for age-appropriate peer interaction was ideal. A typical session takes place on a Saturday or Sunday morning and has approximately 15 teacher candidates and 5–10 community participants with developmental disabilities.

TIES was warmly welcomed by the community participants, their families and the teacher candidates. Each semester, I required the teacher candidates to complete written reflections about their experiences with TIES. In reviewing these reflections, I often found that the teacher candidates articulated revised personal views of normalcy and belonging based on their experiences with the service learning project and the course. Indicating their appreciation of the weekend service-learning project, the teacher candidates for more sessions and the opportunity to continue their participation in the project beyond the requirements of the course. Similarly, community participants and their families had consistently requested more sessions, which was achieved by me teaching another section of the course and doubling the number of sessions offered each semester. It was clear to me that the teacher candidates and community participants were both benefitting from this collaborative integrated endeavor.

6   Unpacking Taylor

The TIES service-learning project that I created seemed like a perfect focus for this chapter. However, as I read more of Taylor's work many emotions passed through me and I found I shifted from cautious optimism at the outset to increasing doubt as I read on and eventually my sentiments could be summed up best with 'it broke my soul.' Suddenly, what I originally believed to be an ideal structure to encourage meaningful interactions with disabled community members in my own university classes now appeared to be a contrived social situation that bore many of the trademarks of the very types of programs that Taylor cautioned against over thirty years ago. At this point, I wasn't sure I could even write this piece and claim progress enacting the ideals Taylor and his contemporaries outlined in their research on community integration. I took a deep breath and pressed on assured by the editors that much could be mined from my project and returned to immersive reading of Taylor's work, hopeful my soul would repair.

My unease centered on the fact that some thirty years had passed since Steven J. Taylor established a set of principles that were intended to guide the decision-making of service providers (Taylor et al., 1987), but these findings were not as central to my project as I might have hoped to find. Following on their review of several model community integration programs nationwide, they developed a set guidelines that advocate (1) all people with developmental disabilities belong in the community, (2) people with severe disabilities should be integrated into typical neighborhoods, work environments, and community settings, (3) social relationships between people with severe disabilities and other people be encouraged, (4) participation in community life be fostered, and (5) people with severe disabilities and their parents be involved in the design, operation, and monitoring of services.

Despite the existence of Taylor et al.'s (1987) clear and logical principles for community integration, structural obstacles have made progress slow, if not impossible. From Taylor's perspective, community integration implies a model of inclusion that weaves together family, friendships, education, meaningful engagement, and necessary support services that spans across an individual's lifetime. Taylor (1988) discusses the residential and special education LRE continuums as structures that direct the placement of individuals with disabilities in locations that range from marginalizing to inclusive. He further explains how significant numbers of people with the most severe disabilities tend to receive their necessary supports in the most restrictive ends of the continuums, both residential and educational. The divisive concepts that Taylor (1988) criticized—restrictive living and learning environments, gatekeeping integrated environments, infringements on basic rights to community participation, and an overall focus on the segregation of people with developmental disabilities rather than the provision of services and supports in integrated settings are all still commonplace and rationalized by the concept of the LRE continuum of placements.

7 A Bridge Too Far?

My discomfort grew as I reviewed my program and saw flaws upon flaws. It was held in a gymnasium, not the community. The activities were largely chosen with limited input from the community participants. In many ways, it was still just a "special" program for people with developmental disabilities. Understanding that the philosophical distance between rationalized segregation (special education) and socially just integration (DSE) represented a seemingly impassable divide, I initially envisioned my project as a bridge—albeit a narrow one—between DSE and special education. However, I now began to wonder if perhaps my task imagined a bridge too far? And would the building of this bridge even be meaningful in an educational system that remained exceedingly resistant to change? Sitting quiet in further reflection on the insights Taylor offered, I processed my own work and came to see the evolution of my flawed service-learning project through a slightly different, unapologetic, Taylorian lens. I could begin to see where TIES might relate.

The college campus is a part of the local community and it is common for members of the local community to participate in events and programs sponsored by the college. It was reasonable to consider TIES as a semi-integrated experience involving teacher candidates and community participants that encouraged social relationships between people with and without developmental disabilities. What we sought with TIES was to carve out a space and time for integration. That, in and of itself, sounds contrived—and in all honesty, it is. The community participants spend most of their days in segregated educational or work environments and many of them know each other from their interactions in other programs for people with developmental disabilities. When we started our collaboration with TIES the main objective was to provide meaningful experiences that would allow the teacher candidates and community participants to interact with and learn from and about each other. Despite the obvious limitations, I felt that we were heading in the right direction—one that Taylor might approve of.

8   Reflections on the Evolution TIES

With this newly acquired Taylorian Lens, I reflected back on the evolution of the TIES service-learning project over the years and the decisions and changes that were made. I realized that my first experience with dissonance and self-doubt began well in advance of working on this chapter. Although I wasn't as familiar with Taylor's work at this time, I had been struggling with and pushing back against some of the very institutional limitations that Taylor identified years ago. Being accustomed to the standards and expectations of teacher education, we (the teacher candidates and I) initially chose and planned activities that the college participants enjoyed and thought the community participants would enjoy, too. The expectation was that the teacher candidates would provide the activities and the community participants would happily participate with them. Once I came to accept this truth I could turn aspects of what the program did on its head and see the flaws with greater clarity.

After the first semester of TIES five years ago, it was evident that the community participants didn't necessarily want to do the activities that we had planned for them. We spent a significant amount of time trying to coerce the community participants into doing things that they might not actually want to do. Some of the community participants indicated their displeasure with the choice of activities by engaging in resistant and challenging behaviors. The teacher candidates made statements about how some of the community participants were challenging or noncompliant at times when they wouldn't participate in a prepared activity. This set up a power dynamic that positioned teacher candidates in a dominant and controlling role, similar to that of a special education teacher who relies on coercion and institutionally sanctioned power to get compliance from their students. This was not how I had envisioned the service-learning project to go. The hoped-for space where the teacher candidates and community participants could get to know each other as individuals and have meaningful interactions failed to evolve as we had instead convened a space of uncertainty and tension. Changes needed to be made—fast.

Activity completion and behavior control had become the de facto goal of the program, and meaningful and engaging communication was not happening. The power dynamic that this created was not much different than a student/teacher school-based relationship and it allowed the teacher candidates to hide behind their activity plans in order to get the participants to complete the activity. I discussed my concerns in class with the teacher candidates and the TIES Program Director and together we brainstormed alternatives to our approach. The first thing we changed was the physical environment. We went from requesting classrooms and small, contained spaces for each separate activity to requesting an open space (a gymnasium) where many activities could be made available at the same time.

The second thing we did was throw away the activity plans. We shifted the focus to providing a number of activity stations and a wide variety of materials that would be made available to all participants. These included: arts & crafts, sports, books, puzzles, board games, nail painting, dancing, and parachute games. The activities were set up each week in the gymnasium and the teacher candidates were no longer expected to teach or run an activity. I spoke to them and explained that they were going to be spending some time with the community participants and their objective should be to communicate and find out what the community participants wanted to do, and then do it with them. If we didn't have anything that a community participant wanted to do, I asked the teacher candidates to figure out what the community participants would like to do and then I would arrange to make that possible. I was trying to remove the power imbalances and create a space for meaningful social peer-integration.

The less we planned the more the participants appeared to be engaged and responsive to meaningful interactions. Without the plan, there was no script for the teacher candidates to follow. They had to figure out how to communicate with the community participants, often in ways other than speech. The teacher candidates were learning how to interpret the actions, gestures and words of the community participants to get to know them and figure out what they wanted, or didn't want, to do. As the power imbalance was reduced and the wishes of the community participants were identified and addressed the atmosphere of the TIES sessions became much more social and less confrontational. The less we tried to control the actions of the community participants, the more meaningful the interactions became.

Back to the present and armed with my ever-deepening understanding of Taylor's work, I continued to critically analyze the TIES program with the help of my teacher candidates. Each week I would talk with them not only about how the weekend program went, but also about concepts that I was really just beginning to think about more critically after studying Taylor's work. I really began to listen to the way that the teacher candidates spoke about their interactions with the community participants. I noticed that the teacher candidates described their interactions with the community participants using language that indicated they viewed their position as authoritative, rather than integrative. This is evident in the opening quote of this chapter where Jillian talked about the 'students' that they 'worked with.' However, this was a common pattern of language in our class discussions and not unique to Jillian. I didn't want the teacher candidates 'working with' community participants or coercing them into doing something they didn't really want to do.

I shared what I was learning about Taylor's work and I spoke to the teacher candidates candidly about the way that their language choice reflected a problematic power differential that made peer interaction nearly impossible. In class, we discussed the importance of getting to know the community participants' strengths, interests, and preferences and how that can positively shape their interactions with them. The deficit-based power-infused language that the teacher candidates used earlier to describe their experiences with the community participants had practically disappeared and was replaced with recognition of their individuality and humanity.

Bogdan and Taylor (1989) were among the early ethnographers to examine how some nondisabled people engage in meaningful, caring, and accepting relationships with people with significant intellectual disabilities to construct them as human. They found that the perspectives of the nondisabled people centered on three common dimensions of humanness: attributing meaningful thinking to the other, seeing individuality in the other, and viewing the other as reciprocating. In examining the teacher candidates' written reflections, each of these dimensions of humanness could be identified in the language as they used to discuss their participation in TIES.

The attribution of meaningful thought to people is important, because in schools and in the community, it is not uncommon to assume that people with significant disabilities are incapable of thinking due to their limitations. It is this line of thought that prevents schools from fully investing in inclusive education, as it seems rational and plausible to consider the intellectual limitations of people with disabilities to be insurmountable. Bogdan and Taylor (1989) found that some people claimed to know what another was thinking despite an absence of typical communication skills involving speech or gestures and differentiated between thinking and communicating thought. Without any observable indication of thinking, people were wont to give the benefit of the doubt to that person and assume the presence of thought. This is essential for future inclusive teachers and the only way to understand this is to have opportunities to interact with people who do not communicate using typical spoken or gestural measures. I could see the attribution of meaningful thought happening and in the words of one of the teacher candidates:

> So, I picked up a basketball and I walked over and I was like Hi Jack my name is Kate do you want to pass around the ball? He was like yeah let's play basketball—in his own way because he's non-verbal and I was like sweet! Here I thought he was going to run away from me and not have a good time but I could tell that he was. Here he was smiling and laughing. (Kate, Teacher Candidate)

One of the primary concepts in my course, 'presuming competence' (Biklen & Burke, 2006), implies that it is always best to assume that an individual is capable of learning and is interested in communicating their preferences or thoughts. However, without opportunities to engage a disabled peer this is little more than a superficial claim.

Seeing individuality in the other is another important way to construct individuals with significant disabilities in a positive light. Seeking to understand people as having distinct personalities likes and dislikes, feelings and motives, life histories, and personal styles that shape their identities. Schools tend to reduce students with disabilities to their classification and strip them of their individuality because of their assumed incompatibility with typical students. By recognizing these aspects of a person's identity, future teachers are able to see commonalities and make connections, which would foster a more inclusive perspective (Bogdan & Taylor, 1989). The teacher candidates were getting an opportunity to see individuality in a way they had never experienced before:

> One aspect of personal growth in my understanding of disability that I took away from this activity was learning how every individual is unique. I feel that it is easy to categorize individuals with disabilities under their classification. For example, one might think that every individual with autism will have the same behaviors, characteristics, or personalities. It can be easy to have pre-existing beliefs about a person with disabilities before you meet them. I can admit that I often did just that. (James, Teacher Candidate)

As a teacher, I will be handed an IEP. This packet tells me everything that I need to know in order to support a child's learning. However, I need to remember that that student is an individual and I can't base all my expectations of them from one piece of paper. As a teacher, I need treat all my students as individuals. They each come into the classroom with unique abilities and skills. Teachers need to build their own understanding of that student on personal interactions and observations. This will better service the child and help create a stronger, more personal relationship with the student. (Maria, Teacher Candidate)

Viewing the other as reciprocating requires that both parties see the other as contributing to the relationship. Bogdan and Taylor (1989) acknowledge that relationships between people with and without disabilities might appear to be one-sided but maintain that nondisabled people in these relationships often report feelings of pleasure, companionship, and accomplishment. The reciprocity of the relationships formed in TIES events became evident as the teacher candidates had time to reflect on their interactions and what it meant for them as future educators:

> I feel that this sense of community I saw in our activity can be created in an academic setting. We created relationships during our TIES activity. I believe that students of all backgrounds can build relationships with each other in the classroom. These relationships are impossible to grow if we segregate our special education and general education students. Schools need to realize how beneficial communities and inclusive classrooms can be. (Carlos, Teacher Candidate)

9   Concluding Thoughts and Lingering Doubts

As I talk to new groups of teacher candidates each semester, I see the ongoing and urgent need to continue my work to break down the boundaries that society has built up between people with and without disabilities. I find myself relying more and more upon DSE insights to point my students to this ideology and provide them with the language to articulate their thoughts and criticisms. Late in my research I found an article by Taylor that seemed to get right to the heart of the matter by naming something that sounds so simple, but yet eludes so many—constructing humanness. Taylor (1989) identified constructing humanness as a precursor to full community integration and by extension, I believe that it is also required for meaningful inclusive education.

> Whether or not people with severe disabilities will be treated as human beings or persons is not a matter of their physical or mental condition. It is a matter of definition. We can show that they, and we, are human by including, by accepting them rather than separating them out. (Bogdan & Taylor, 1989, p. 146)

I shared the concept of constructing humanness with my class and we talked about how this related to their experiences with the community participants and the implications for them as future educators. Through the service learning project, the teacher candidates were given opportunities to have meaningful social interactions with people with developmental disabilities, while mitigating challenging power imbalances and ultimately constructing humanness in the community participants—something that typical field experiences, and society, do not readily provide a space for.

Viewing the TIES service-learning project through a Taylorian lens, although painful at times, has given me a more critically informed understanding of the project and my teaching. The structural limitations of special education are fueled by deeply engrained socio-cultural understandings and assumptions about disability and have created an unimaginable force that has been resistant to change for almost 40 years. For a modicum of validation, I reflect back to the beginning of this chapter where I cited Taylor et al.'s (1987) acknowledgement that paradigmatic change takes place slowly, if at all. That given the resistance of the structure to change, somewhat less integrated or stopgap settings can be unapologetically viable options. With posthumous permission from Taylor assumed, I do see the value of TIES for the community participants, teacher candidates and myself. I continue to challenge my teacher candidates and myself on a regular basis to make progress, albeit slow progress, on the very topics that Taylor elucidated on so pointedly and passionately.

Despite the slow turning wheels of progress, the teacher candidates leave my class with new, yet still under-developed, understandings of special education, inclusion, and disability. I see change in the teacher candidates over each semester even though we continue to work within the very system that reproduces the narratives that maintain these gaps. Some days, this makes actual progress seem almost impossible. But Taylor knew progress would likely remain imperfect for some time.

> We do know, however, that good people across the country are doing good things for people with the most severe disabilities. They are committed to community integration and are providing answers to some of the things we do not know. They are making community integration work, not perfectly perhaps, but making it work nonetheless. This much we know. (Taylor et al. 1987, p. 53)

With those parting words from Steven Taylor, I hope that I will continue to be dissatisfied with my progress, and yet, always at the ready to seek new solutions, and work within the spaces I can fortify to build my bridge—one semester, one community participant, one teacher candidate at a time.

Notes

1 I have recently come across an introductory special education textbook edited by Meyen and Skrtic (1995) that does just what I am trying to do by dedicating half of the text understanding alternative perspectives on the professionalism of special education, the sociology of disability, socio-cultural factors that influence disability, and discussion of the failures of special education as a justification of widespread school reform. This text was first published in 1978 and last in 1995 and I am left wondering why it was discontinued and mourning its loss.
2 Additionally, the prioritization of equity, diversity, and inclusion initiatives by College administration has provided a space where my DSE work is not only valued but has room to grow within and beyond my department. I am an active part of a nascent professional exchange on campus that involves the collaboration of faculty from various disciplines working together to provide professional development and education on issues related to racial justice and supporting the LGBTQAI* community, as well as understanding ableism and promoting the inclusion of people with disabilities. Another short-term goal of this exchange is the creation of an interdisciplinary certificate or minor in Disability Studies that would be open to all students, regardless of major.

References

Ashby, C. (2012). Disability studies and inclusive teacher preparation: A socially just path for teacher education. *Research & Practice for Persons with Severe Disabilities*, 37(2), 89–99.

Ashton, J. R. (2011). The CEC professional standards: A Foucauldian genealogy of the re/construction of special education. *International Journal of Inclusive Education, 15*(8), 775–795.

Biklen, D., & Burke, J. (2006). Presuming competence. *Equity & Excellence in Education, 39*(2), 166–175.

Bogdan, R., & Taylor, S. J. (1989). Relationships with severely disabled people: The social construction of humanness. *Social Problems, 36*(2), 135–146.

Brantlinger, E. A. (Ed.). (2006). *Who benefits from special education: Remediating (fixing) other people's children*. Lawrence Erlbaum Associates.

Danforth, S. (2017). *Becoming a great inclusive educator*. Peter Lang.

Lalvani, P., & Broderick, A. A. (2013). Institutionalized ableism and the misguided "disability awareness day": Transformative pedagogies for teacher education. *Equity & Excellence in Education, 46*(4), 468–483.

Meyen, E. L., & Skrtic, T. M. (1995). *Special education and student disability: Traditional, emerging, and alternative perspectives*. Love Publishing.

Nisbet, J. (2004). Commentary: "Caught in the Continuum." *Research and Practice for Persons with Severe Disabilities, 29*(4), 321–236.

Orsati, F. (2016). Humanistic practices to understand and support students' behaviors: A disability studies in education framework. In M. Cosier & C. Ashby (Eds.), *Enacting change from within: Disability studies meets teaching and teacher education*. Peter Lang.

Rice, N. (2006). Promoting 'epistemic fissures': Disability studies in teacher education. *Teaching Education, 17*(3), 251–264.

Sapon-Shevin, M. (2014). How we respond to differences—And the difference it makes. In D. Lawrence-Brown & M. Sapon-Shevin (Eds.), *Condition critical: Key principles for equitable and inclusive education* (pp. 17–32). Teachers College Press.

Slee, R. (1998). The politics of special education. In C. Clark, A. Dyson, & A. Millward (Eds.), *Theorizing special education* (pp. 30–41). Routledge.

Slee, R. (2001). Social justice and the changing directions in educational research: The case of inclusive education. *International Journal of Inclusive Education, 5*(2–3), 167–177.

Slesaransky-Poe, G., & Garcia, A. M. (2014). The social construction of difference. In D. Lawrence-Brown & M. Sapon-Shevin (Eds.), *Condition critical: Key principles for equitable and inclusive education* (pp. 66–85). Teachers College Press.

Smith, R. (2014). Considering behavior as meaningful communication. In D. Lawrence-Brown & M. Sapon-Shevin (Eds.), *Condition critical: Key principles for equitable and inclusive education* (pp. 154–168). Teachers College Press.

Stringfellow, J. L., & Edmonds-Behrend, C. (2013). Service learning: Extending the classroom to the community. *Delta Kappa Gamma Bulletin, 79*(3), 42–45.

Taylor, S. J. (1988). Caught in the continuum: a critical analysis of the principle of the least restrictive environment. *Journal of the Association for Persons with Severe Handicaps, 13*(1), 45–53.

Taylor, S. J. (2009). *Acts of conscience: World War II, mental institutions, and religious objectors.* Syracuse University Press.

Taylor, S. J. (2011). Disability studies in higher education. *New Directions for Higher Education, 154,* 93–98.

Taylor, S. J., Racino, J. A., Knoll, J. A., & Lutifyya, Z. (1987). *The nonrestrictive environment: On community integration for people with the most severe disabilities.* Human Policy Press.

Turnbull, H. R. (Ed.). (1981). *The least restrictive alternative: Principles and practices.* American Association on Mental Deficiency.

Valle, J., & Connor, D. (2011). *Rethinking disability: A disability studies approach to inclusive practices.* McGraw-Hill.

Ware, L. (2001). Writing, identity, and the other: Dare we do disability studies? *Journal of Teacher Education, 52*(2), 107–123.

Ware, L. (2004). *Ideology and the politics of (in)exclusion.* Peter Lang.

Index

abuse   4, 7, 51, 70, 75, 80, 87, 88
advocacy   1–3, 16, 45, 49, 53, 76, 80, 82, 85, 89
Arendt, H.   21
Ashton, J.   10, 91
autism   16, 42, 68–70, 75, 76, 103

behaviour/behavior   IX, 30, 31, 33, 42, 44, 50, 56, 95, 100, 103
Beratan, G.   44
Berger, P. L.   4, 82
Biklen, D.   VII, 1, 2, 8, 10, 22, 45, 75, 80
Blatt, B.   10, 75, 80
Bogdan, R.   7, 10, 20, 30, 75, 80, 82–85, 87–89, 102, 103
Brantlinger, E.   VII, 8

Campbell, F. K.   67
career   VII, IX, XII, 8, 10, 21, 80, 87, 88, 93, 94
Carlson, L.   33
case studies   75, 82
Center on Human Policy   2, 3, 65, 75, 80, 81, 85
Child Protective Service (CPS)   87
Connor, D. J.   14, 15, 18
critical disability studies   17, 18, 22
culture   18, 24, 44, 73

Danforth, S.   15, 37, 89
Davies, B.   66
Deleuze, G.   68
deviance   5, 13, 14, 45, 67, 81, 82, 84
difference   18, 21, 31, 32, 34, 42, 44–47, 67, 69, 74, 76, 84, 85, 95, 96
disability studies   VII–X, 1–10, 13–23, 25, 29, 30, 33, 49, 65, 71, 74, 75, 77, 94, 105
Disability Studies in Education (DSE)   VII–X, 1, 2, 5, 7–9, 13, 14, 17–19, 22, 29, 77, 94
Doris, J.   39

Education for All Handicapped Children Act (EHA/EHC)   36, 37, 39, 40, 49
ethical   18, 33, 88
ethnography/ethnographic   4, 5, 13, 15, 70

family   5, 6, 13, 15, 16, 31, 54, 70, 71, 75, 83–87, 98

Foucault, M.   23
Freire, P.   68

Gallagher, D.   18
Goffman, E.   4, 81, 82
Goodley, D.   16, 17, 20, 21
Guattari, F.   68

Hacking, I.   16, 17, 19, 20, 22
Hartley, D.   19
Hehir, T.   51
humanness   9, 20, 30, 68, 75, 83, 89, 102, 104

ideology   IX, 10, 73, 104
inclusive education   IX, 9, 37, 38, 41, 42, 52, 55, 89, 102, 104
Individualized Education Plan (IEP)   38, 40, 42, 45, 46, 50, 87, 93, 103
Individuals With Disabilities Act (IDEA)/ Individuals With Disabilities Education Act (IDEIA)   7, 9, 37, 40, 41, 44, 47, 49, 52, 55, 56
institutions   1, 5, 7, 8, 10, 15, 16, 21, 22, 24, 25, 31, 39, 43, 49, 55, 67, 68, 73, 75, 77, 80–83, 88
intellectual disability   30, 31, 33, 36, 37, 42, 43, 45–49, 51–53, 57, 70, 87
inter-regnum   13, 19

Jorgensen, C. M.   9, 36, 37

Kliewer, C.   8, 45

label(s)   16, 30, 31, 42, 45, 52, 75, 77, 80–84, 86–89, 96
Latour, B.   21
Least Restrictive Environment (LRE)   7, 9, 36–41, 43–55, 57, 93, 96, 98
Linton, S.   13, 21
Luckman, T.   82

McRuer, R.   67
Mental Retardation (journal)   9, 65, 75
Moll, L.   45

neglect   5, 87
Nussbaum, M.   25

Oliver, M. 15

Palley, E. 40, 55
possibility 8, 29, 32, 38, 39, 66, 93
power VII–IX, 13, 14, 22, 24, 30–32, 44, 49, 66, 67, 71, 74–76, 100, 101, 104
principles 7, 15, 25, 37, 43, 53, 65, 85, 86, 98
privilege IX, 21, 22, 24, 44, 45, 49, 50, 67, 69, 95
Public Law 94-142, 39

race 24, 45, 48, 49
Rice, N. 2, 3, 10, 80
Rosenau, N. 74

Sarason, S. 39
segregation 7, 14, 15, 37–39, 42, 43, 55, 57, 59, 67, 91–94, 98, 99
Shakespeare, T. 15

Smith, P. 47, 48, 71–73
social security 87
special education VII–IX, 1, 2, 5, 7, 10, 13–15, 18, 31, 38–40, 42, 44–49, 51, 54–56, 77, 89, 91, 93–100, 103–105
stories 24, 71, 72, 82, 83
Story Sauer, J. 1, 36
Supreme Court Brown v. Board of Education of Topeka (1954) 38

Taylor, S. VII, VIII, 1–10, 13–16, 19, 20, 22, 25, 29–34, 36, 37, 57, 65–68, 70, 71, 74–77, 80–85, 87–89, 91–93, 97–105
The Dukes/Duke family 16, 32, 86, 87
transformation 2, 10, 37, 54, 55, 66, 67

Valle, J. 20

Ware, L. 1, 20, 22

Printed in the United States
by Baker & Taylor Publisher Services